Good Dog Dandy

Other books by Malcolm Saville in Armada

The Brown Family series

The Secret of Galleybird Pit
The Roman Treasure Mystery

Lone Pine series

Mystery at Witchend
Seven White Gates
The Gay Dolphin Adventure
The Secret of Grey Walls
Lone Pine Five
The Elusive Grasshopper
The Neglected Mountain
Saucers Over the Moor
Wings Over Witchend
Not Scarlet But Gold
Treasure at Amorys
Man With Three Fingers
Rye Royal
Strangers at Witchend

Buckingham series

The Master of Maryknoll
The Long Passage

Good Dog Dandy

Malcolm Saville

An Armada Original

First published in 1971 by
Wm. Collins Sons & Co. Ltd.,
14 St. James's Place, London S.W.1.

Printed in Great Britain by
Love & Malcomson Ltd.,
Brighton Road, Redhill, Surrey.

Foreword

THE places in which this story is set are real, although I have not called them by the names you will find on the map. If you are ever lucky enough to come to Sussex, you may recognise the town I call Malling which has stood for hundreds of years where a muddy, tidal river slips through the valley it has made on its way to the sea twelve miles away. Here, to guard this gap in the South Downs, William the Conqueror built a mighty castle the walls of which still tower above the red-roofed town and up which Lucinda Jane and her brother climbed on the first day of the summer holidays at the beginning of this surprising adventure. So far as I know there is no café in Malling called *"Four & Twenty Blackbirds."*

None of the people in the story are real nor is Dandy the Police Dog, but there are sure to be many dogs like him working hard wherever you live, to help you and your friends and the police and to stop things going wrong.

So now is the time for me to say "Thank you" to the Sussex Constabulary for helping me to tell you a little of how these splendid dogs are trained—they go to a special school with the police officers with whom they live—and to say how much I enjoyed going out with them to watch their training and see them at work.

This story is complete in itself, but readers who would like to know how the Browns arrived at Malling and opened the *"Four & Twenty Blackbirds"* and met their new friends can read their first adventure in

"The Secret of Galleybird Pit". A Regency snuff-box like that described in this story can be seen in the Royal Pavilion at Brighton.

M.S.
Seaford,
Sussex. 1970.

The People in the Story

Lucinda Jane Brown	Age 12
Humphrey (Humf) Brown	her brother, age 9
Mary Brown Mervyn Brown	Their parents, who are newcomers to Malling where they own and run a small café called *"Four & Twenty Blackbirds"*
Elsie	who helps in the café
John & Peggy Hogben	(13 and 12) and their parents who are farmers
Mark Simson	Age 12. The vicar's son
Betsy Maycock	Age 12
Police Sergeant Harry Maycock	her father, and Dandy's 'Handler'
Police Sergeant Carter	The local station officer
P.C. Bill Harris P.C. Robert Pinder	The panda crew
Mr. & Mrs. Strang	Turkey farmers at Pollards
Jasper	A ne'er-do-well
Miss Sandford	An artist

1

Tuesday: Private Business

THERE are few more exciting days in the year than that on which school breaks up for the summer holidays.

On the Tuesday at the end of July on which this story opens, Lucinda Jane Brown who came to live in Malling from the midlands only six months ago, was talking to her friends John and Peggy Hogben outside the school gates. Hundreds of other chattering boys and girls streamed past them full of exciting plans for the weeks ahead and it was difficult to make herself heard.

Lucy, as everybody called her, was twelve. She was small for her age, with straight, fair hair, falling to her shoulders which she nearly always kept in place with a blue band. Her eyes were blue and her nose was nearly snub and when she smiled she looked as pretty as she was nice.

She was smiling now while John protested that there wasn't time now to listen to gossipping girls when they were all going to meet tomorrow at their farm called Conways about three miles away in the Downs.

"Don't be in such a hurry today," Lucy pleaded. "I know you'll be busy helping your dad on the farm and we don't suppose you'll have a moment to talk to us for weeks, but I enjoy feeling excited about breaking up after our first term here and just for once I don't want to rush home."

John Hogben was six inches taller than either of the girls, and there was nothing he wanted more in life than to farm Conways with his father and ride horses whenever he could. School was something to be dealt with as soon as possible. He was usually untidily dressed, very tanned, with grey eyes and straight, bleached hair with a lock that often fell over his forehead.

"O.K. little Lucy," he grinned. "You stay here thinking about how wonderful everything is going to be, and if you're not over at Conways tomorrow we'll come back here and remind you where you ought to be. I suppose you've got to bring Humf? . . . Hullo. Here's Mark. Pity he can't come too."

Mark Simson was the vicar's son and an old friend of the Hogbens and had been kind to the Browns as soon as they had arrived as strangers in Malling. Lucy liked John although he did sometimes try to be rather superior, but Mark was the best boy friend of her short life. She was also aware that Peggy, with whom she now got on well enough, had known Mark longer and never allowed him to forget it.

"That's enough of that term that was," he remarked. "How are the famous 'Blackbirds' Lucy? Not too broody, I hope. Haven't been in lately. And where's Humf? And has your father, who I like very much, had any more bright ideas?"

Before Lucy could answer, Peggy broke in.

"Must you really go with your parents tomorrow, Mark? Wish you could come with us. Although John's always pretending that Dad can't do any work on the farm without him, we had an idea last night, and if all the parents agree and the weather stays O.K., we could go camping down at the sea at Greenhaven or maybe on the Strang's farm on the edge of the forest . . ."

"Why didn't you tell us that before, Peggy?" Lucy gasped. "It's a marvellous idea."

"Hoped we might persuade Mark to come too. More fun if we could all go together. Any hope, Mark?"

He looked at the two girls shrewdly.

"Not this week, Peg. You know I'm going with the parents in our caravan, and we were due to go tomorrow, but now Dad's got a funeral at the end of the week. I can't leave them now and there's lots I can do to help at home. We'll fix something with Lucy and Humf when I come back. Plenty of time yet and I expect we shall go on Saturday or Monday now. I'm keen on the forest idea and never met the Strangs at Pollards. My father told me he's a very interesting chap, but there's no reason why you shouldn't go first. So long, all. Be a good girl, Lucy and give my love to your mother and tell her we'll come in and see her and enjoy some of her cakes before we go."

Lucy hoped that he'd look back and wave but he didn't, and she was still watching him go down the hill when she saw her brother sauntering up towards them.

Humphrey Mervyn Brown was nine and still at another school. He was a tough little boy. Sandy and freckled with big, innocent grey eyes that misled people until they knew him better. He was called Humf by everyone, except by a few respectable and distant relations. A sort of puffing, grunting 'humf' was the first word he spoke and he adopted it as his own particular means of communication and often pretended not to hear when he was called Humphrey. He had never been able to persuade his teacher that Humf was anything but a rudish noise but it was only occasionally that his father Mervyn, when in one of his moods, insisted that Humphrey was the name to which he should answer.

John and Peggy thought at first, and with some reason, that he was inclined to be cheeky, but they soon accepted him for Lucy's sake and recognised that he was loyal, brave and cheerful. John was also aware that the little boy had long ago accepted him as his particular hero.

Humf welcomed them with a broad grin.

"Hullo! I've broke up too. I thought we ought to do something special this morning like a special, greedy sort of ice, and thanks very much for waiting for me."

"But we weren't waiting for you, little man," Peggy said. "We're just going, but our Mum and Dad who spoil you, say that maybe when you come over to Conways tomorrow we might take you camping by the sea."

"In a tent?" Humf asked doubtfully. "One of those small green tents you have to lie flat in? By myself? Have we asked our father, Lucy? He's in a rather peculiar mood and excited about us doing something special on Mum's birthday on Saturday. If what you say is really true. If you swear a noath about it, I s'pose you know this is almost the most smashing thing that ever happened to me . . . You mean sleep out all night? Every night until we go home for Mum's birthday on Saturday? That's three nights."

"That's right, Humf boy," John promised. "Three nights in the same tent as me, and if you snore or wake me up or ask silly questions I'll throw you out."

"And what happens if I just happen to breathe?" Humf suggested cheekily as he dodged John's avenging hand. "Thanks very much all the same, John and Peggy. I'll be a useful camper, I swear."

"Cheerio for now then," Peggy said. "If Mum's coming into town in the car in the morning she'll pick you up. If she hasn't arrived by eleven you must telephone us. Must say it will help when they get the *Blackbirds* connected. Don't forget to bring your swimming things . . . Now we must rush and you'd better practice sleeping without breathing, Humf."

At first the two Browns had not much liked Peggy who was slim and dark and wore spectacles. She had been jealous because Mark had befriended Lucy and Humf who had felt shy and strange when they had first come to Malling and knew nothing about farming or what happened in the country. But Lucy, who was generous, and quick to admit what she didn't know, and who always championed her young brother, soon won over Peggy and took no notice of her sharp tongue.

So when the two Hogbens had fetched their bikes, Lucy called 'goodbye' to a few more friends and walked off with her brother. The rooms above the *Blackbirds* in which the Browns had made their new home were in Pottery Lane, off the High Street which was dominated by the keep of the great Norman castle. As the fine new school was down by the river it took Lucy twice as long to walk home as to run down. Humf's school was much nearer the café and she was wondering why he had come to meet her, when she remembered that their mother had gone off to Brighton for a day's shopping. This meant that *Blackbirds* was in their father's charge. He prided himself on being a man of ideas, but was not fond of work. And, of course, there was Elsie who came every day and could never do enough for them.

Lucy was old enough to realise that without her mother the café would soon close. She knew that they had come to Malling because Mervyn had failed in business in Midchester. She was also aware that in spite of his irritating ways, he was kind and really loved them all. He was always hoping and planning exciting things for them. He liked nothing better than to take them on expeditions. He called history the story of vanished men and so made it exciting. He liked reading to them, even at meals, when their mother was in a hurry; he had crazes like wanting to paint and make pottery to sell in the shop, and Lucy knew that there were times when he was so thoughtless that he made their mother cry. But Humf, in his funny, silent way, had never failed with his sister to help their mother. Lucy did not intend to have him made fun of by John and Peggy—or even by Mark who had no brothers nor sisters.

Humf stopped outside the window of a small shop which sold sports gear and looked longingly at three fishing rods.

"Has Dad promised to take you fishing?" Lucy asked suspiciously. "He can't go today while Mum's away. Did you go home after you broke up or come to meet me? Humf, is everything O.K. at the café?"

"I just popped in. Dad was upstairs and nobody was eating or drinking or anything so Elsie gave me a lolly . . . I like Elsie. Then I thought I'd like to tell you something, Lucy. It's private. It's something I'm going to do, but now John says all this about camping out tomorrow. Is it real? Does Dad know?"

Lucy nodded. "I think so, Humf. You won't be silly if you come, will you? . . . And has Dad promised to take you fishing?"

"Not yet, he hasn't," Humf admitted, "but I think he will. He says there are lots of important things we've all got to do together in the summer but that we'll discuss—that's what he says when he means talk about—he says we'll discuss after Mum's birthday on Saturday which is very special and he's got plans."

This was a long speech for Humf, and Lucy knew that he had not yet said what he really wanted to tell her. She knew that they would only be allowed to go to Conways until Saturday because that was their mother's birthday, and anyway they wouldn't want to be anywhere else but with her on that day.

"O.K. Humf," she said. "Let's go up to the castle as it's the first day of the holidays and you can tell me your private thing. We'll have to do something about Mum's birthday but I haven't got much money. Maybe we'll have to try to earn something, somehow. And I can tell you something else, Humf. You won't make any money by selling the fish you won't catch because you can't afford a rod."

"My plans aren't fish," Humf said smugly. "They're the sort of plans that could change all our plans. Actually, Lucy, they could change my life when I'm a bit older.

Lucy didn't laugh at him.

"Come on then, Humf. Let's share another secret. I hope there's nobody in our special place where we can see down into the little garden where the people look like dwarfs. And don't worry about the fishing. Mark will teach you when he comes back in a fortnight . . . And we mustn't be long now because without Mum we can help a bit in the kitchen when people come in at dinner-time."

So they climbed up the steep, worn stone stairs of the keep of the castle and Lucy, as she always did, tried to imagine what the Norman soldiers in their mail would have looked like as they clanked up these very steps. They would have looked down the river sliding between its muddy banks to the narrow sea which the first Normans had come to England across and won a bloody battle against a brave English king called Harold at a hill called Senlac only a few miles away. And perhaps one of these proud soldiers in a foreign land had stood where Humf and she were standing now and wondered how his wife and children were faring in the green pastures of Normandy. And Lucy suddenly knew why her romantic and unpractical father was moved and excited by thoughts like this, and if there was nothing else he could do for them all he, more than anybody, would show them what was beautiful and remind them always of the deeds of those vanished men and women and of what they had done to enrich the lives of others.

Lucy couldn't have put such thoughts into those words at that moment, while she stood with her brother and looked down into the courtyard of the castle which was now a grassy little garden in which somebody had thoughtfully set a few seats for visitors.

"Now tell me your secret, Humf, because we mustn't be long. You're sure it's not about Mum? I mean, we know she's tired and working too hard and can't have a holiday yet, but you haven't heard anything else awful about her and Dad not helping properly have you? Or about Elsie?"

Humf's hands were grasping the top bar of the iron railing over which he was barely tall enough to look even on tiptoe. He shook his head and then remarked surprisingly, "It happened to me yesterday at school. It's nothing to do with Dad or Mum. I'm going to be a policeman with a dog. A dog like Dandy."

Humf, like most small boys, often surprised his family with ideas for his future. He had not been particularly keen on flying round the moon after seeing the brave astronauts on television. He had been bored when his father had told him he was old enough to watch cricket and taken him to see Sussex play at Hove. Because he admired John Hogben and liked animals he had talked for several weeks about being a farmer, but a policeman was a new idea.

"What's a dog got to do with it, Humf and who's Dandy?"

"I s'pose they don't do interesting things like showing you police dogs at your school, Lucy. That's bad luck for you. We had a policeman and a fantastic dog called Dandy yesterday. I can tell you I had a jolly long talk with the policeman after. This one's name is Harry and he's a sergeant which is higher than a constable. All the time he looks after Dandy whó lives at his home and he's got a girl who goes to your school and I talked to Dandy and I can tell you that if he doesn't like you he's very fierce. He's as big as a wolf and looks like one. Sergeant Harry says now that I've spoken to Dandy and stroked him he'll be my friend for life. Did you know that Dandy helps people like us and the police all the time? It's his job. Did you know that, Lucy? I didn't say anything about all this last night 'cos I wanted to think about it. Now I know that's what I'm going to be. Sergeant Harry told me that they want chaps like me when we're big enough and so I thought I'd like to tell you about it. I haven't told Mum and Dad or Elsie."

Lucy knew that specially trained policeman did come to schools to talk about their work and of how important it was to go to them if you were in trouble. At her last school she remembered lessons on kerb drill which she had never forgotten.

"But what do the dogs do, Humf? Do they chase burglars?"

"I s'pect they do, Lucy. The important thing that sergeant told us, is that we can help Dandy as much as he can help us. He gave us all a comic too. I got it here. Everyone in the class had one and you can see it if you like. It's got pictures of Dandy on it."

The crumpled sheet of yellow paper which Humf took from his pocket didn't look much like a comic, but when Lucy unfolded it she saw that it was headed 'Calling All Children'. It did have picture stories like a comic of an alsatian dog called Dandy sharing some adventures with a boy and girl after explaining that he was a police dog. Humf, who was a good, quick reader, showed Lucy how Dandy and all the boys and girls could help each other. First the dog explained that the first way for children to help him was *never* to go for a ride in a car driven by anybody they didn't know, but to run home as fast as they could and try to remember the number of the car.

"You see, Lucy, that it's jolly important to help a dog like Dandy and the policeman he works for," Humf explained. "It's real detective work. Honestly it is. Sergeant Harry said it doesn't matter if you're only just nine so long as you can remember car numbers and what some people look like. Policemen want to know things like that and I'm going to practice all the time . . . See the next picture where Dandy says never to take sweets or ices from somebody we don't know. I've often wished somebody would give me an ice and Harry said it doesn't matter if it's a friend or a relation, but if it's somebody we've never seen before, we're to run home or tell somebody we do know about the stranger. He didn't say why, but I s'pose the ices are poisoned or something peculiar . . . Now see what Dandy says about boys and girls helping him. He says we must try to remember what the man or woman looked like and what they were wearing, 'cos if we can remember that will save Dandy hours and hours of hard work . . . And here's another thing which doesn't matter so much now because it's summer time and light outside when we go to bed, but Dandy says that if we're by ourselves we're not to go exploring in the dark with anybody we don't know who asks us the way . . ."

Lucy looked at him affectionately. He was a funny little boy and often made them all laugh, but she knew now that he was serious and that it would be most unfair to make fun of him. And she was also old enough to know that what Dandy had told the children at school would help them to remember something they should know.

"Pity we haven't got room in the *Blackbirds* for a dog like Dandy," Humf said. "I shall have to tell Mum and Dad soon about me going to be a policeman because it might mean a lot of extra work for me, but I wanted to tell you first. Before John or Mark even."

"Thank you very much, Humf. But why?"

"I knew you wouldn't laugh or say wait until I'm old enough. I'd like you to meet Dandy. There isn't anything I want to do more when I'm old enough except be a policeman and work with Dandy. I s'pose that's not much good though 'cos Dandy will be too old to wait for me and he'll be dead."

Lucy knew that there was no answer to this question which could satisfy Humf, so she turned with her back to the railings and passed him the Dandy comic.

"Thank you for showing me, Humf. I'd like to meet Dandy too and I've just thought of something. Can you remember Sergeant Harry's other name. There's a girl at school called Betsy Maycock. I don't know her but somebody told me that her dad's a policeman."

Humf shook his head. "I don't think they said his name except that he was a handler. I think that's because he handles Dandy all the time and went to this special school with him. Dandy won't do anything that anyone else but Harry tells him. He just won't. Harry speaks so quietly to him we couldn't hear what he says. Sometimes he says that Dandy knows what he's thinking which is a super sort of magic thing . . . Anyway, what about this Betsy girl?"

"If your Sergeant Harry is her dad, then Dandy would live in their home, wouldn't he?"

"You mean you could be friends with her and then take me round to meet Dandy properly and p'raps I could learn to do detective things with him? You do that thing, Lucy. Ask Peggy or somebody if she knows the girl. We'll ask her when we go to Conways tomorrow but let's keep it all a secret because Mum is worried just now, and Dad might say he wanted to start a farm of dogs like Dandy and give up the *Blackbirds*."

While her brother was making these shrewd comments, Lucy heard the murmur of voices from the grassy courtyard far below them.

Two men were sitting on one of the seats with their backs to the castle walls, and although they were too far away to hear what they were saying, Lucy believed that the elder was their father.

Mervyn Brown was an unusual-looking man. He was slim and dark with a lined, tanned face and striking grey eyes. In spite of his wife's protests, he usually wore something which made other people look twice at him. He liked dark blue shirts with which he would wear a gaily coloured, floral tie and was once particularly pleased when he overheard somebody in the café remark that he looked like an artist. For a few months he had enjoyed a craze for wearing unusual hats and had, in turn, surprised them with a bright blue beret—this must have been after the comment about the artist—followed by a fisherman's tweed hat and then, for a few weeks, a cap with earflaps which he bought at a jumble sale organised by the ladies of the church of which Mark's father was the vicar. Once, during this lovely summer, he had sported a yellowish straw panama but Pickwick, their cat, had sharpened her claws on it and so, now, he was hatless.

"Look, Humf," Lucy whispered. "I'm sure that's Dad down there, but who's the other man? Have you seen him before? Was he there when you just popped in to the *Blackbirds* to gorge yourself?"

"I'm not a gorger, Lucy, and I've never seen that

other man. I expect he got talking to Dad in the café and said something about the castle and so Dad said, 'My dear sir. This castle of ours was built by the Normans. It is the pride of our town. Allow me to show it to you,' and there he is doing that thing."

Lucy giggled. Humf's deep voice was not much like his father's but they had both often heard him speak to strangers in just such a pompous way, and it was true that however busy their mother or Elsie might be, Mervyn would walk out with any stranger who showed an interest in the town and spend the next half hour with him whether he'd bought anything in the café or not.

Suddenly she was angry.

"But Humf, he's left Elsie alone in the *Blackbirds*! There's nobody to help her. We must run and I'm going to tell Dad that he must come as well. Elsie can't cook *and* serve and I don't care who that man is."

"He doesn't know we're here," Humf whispered. "Look, Lucy! Dad's new friend is showing him something he's taken out of his pocket. I wonder what it is. Let's ask him."

"We can't do that, but we can remind Dad that Mother won't be back yet and that he must come and help in the café."

But as she hurried down the steps she feared something that she didn't want to mention to her brother. Mervyn Brown was hopeless about money. Time and again she had heard her mother beg him not to spend on presents for them all or take them on expensive expeditions until the *Blackbirds* was really going well. Her father could nearly always be persuaded to buy something he couldn't afford and didn't actually need and by the way in which he had been examining the small article which his companion had taken from his pocket, Lucy feared the worst. Humf didn't say much but he seemed to know what she was thinking. He was an astute little boy.

The steps were too worn and steep to run down, and by the time they reached ground level Mervyn and his companion were disappearing under the old archway into the street.

"Hullo, Dad!" Humf shouted as he ran after them ahead of Lucy, and as both men turned in surprise the children saw their father's companion for the first time. He was youngish with long, unkempt reddish hair and side whiskers and his eyes were hidden with sun specs. He was wearing tight blue jeans and the sort of brightly coloured, patterned shirt that Lucy guessed would inspire her father to buy something similar before long.

The young man slowly removed his sun glasses and stared at them as though he hated the sight of children. Then, with a word and a brief nod to Mervyn he turned and hurried out into the town.

"Hullo, Dad," Humf said again. "We were up in the tower having a private talk and saw you. We've both broke up. Who was that man who didn't like us? I can't see why people shouldn't like us if they don't know us."

"Of course I know you have both started your summer holidays today," Mervyn said without enthusiasm. "And you don't say 'Broke up,' Humphrey. You say 'Broken up,' although that is a ridiculous phrase. And what, might I ask, are you both doing up in the castle at this time of day? Surely you can find something more useful to do?"

Lucy was near tears. "But Dad, have you really left Elsie alone? You promised Mother this morning that you would stay in the café until she came back from Brighton. You know you did. We heard you. Is she back already, and who was that man who was showing you something out of his pocket? I hate asking questions like this, Dad, but can't you see how awful it would be if Elsie walked out and left us because there's nobody to help her. You promised Mum. Don't be cross with us, please. We want to help too. Specially as Mum is having a day off. And why don't you tell us about the young man? Do we know him?"

"It should not be necessary for me to explain my actions to my children," Mervyn said in the voice he used when he hated answering questions. "As however you seem to have been spying on me, I can inform you that I am now going back to the *Blackbirds* and that the matter I have been discussing with that young man is confidential. Should you be unaware of the meaning of that word, Humphrey, I must explain that it means private. It concerns business which I can only conduct by myself and not in the presence of Elsie . . . That is enough, Lucinda. Your mother has not returned and I must ask you not to refer again to the subject of my recent meeting and conversation. Have I made myself clear?"

"O.K. by us," Humf said doubtfully. "All the same, we'd like to know why that chap didn't want to speak to us. And we weren't spying. I just happened to be discussing with Lucy about my plans and there you were sitting down here just as if you had a secret."

"Look after Humf," Lucy said to her father. "I'm going to run ahead to help Elsie. It's horrible of you to have left her alone when Mother isn't here."

Pottery Lane was an old, narrow street leading off the High Street in the centre of the town. On one side was a row of little bright, clean houses with gay coloured doors and on the other a few shops with the *Four & Twenty Blackbirds* at the top with the name painted in black on a hanging sign of bright orange.

Above the windows, where the name of the owner is usually printed, was painted a row of sitting, walking, hopping, flying blackbirds. Lucy, brushing the tears from her eyes, opened the shop door and saw with dismay a rather grumpy looking couple sitting without anything to eat at one table, and an even crosser-looking woman reading a newspaper at another.

After her mother, Elsie was the kindest woman Lucy had ever known. She was big and fresh-faced and jolly and when she wasn't chattering she was laughing. She had worked in the café before the Browns had bought it, helped them repaint it and settle in, kept it clean, waited on customers and cooked simple meals when Mrs. Brown wasn't there, and made a fuss of Humf when she had the chance. The family's fear was that she might leave them when she got a home of her own and married her Bill which, on the rare occasions when she was a little put out at the *Blackbirds*, she suggested might be within the next few weeks.

As soon as Lucy pushed back the kitchen door, she knew there was trouble. The room was full of smoke and the smell of burning toast as Elsie broke eggs into the metal poacher on the stove.

"I'm that pleased to see you, love," Elsie gasped. "Start the toast again there's a good girl while I take those miseries out there something to get them started. I never did like that toaster and it's jammed again. Four pairs of hands I haven't got and I can't be in the kitchen and out there looking after people who only want what we haven't got."

"I'm *so* sorry, Elsie," Lucy gasped. "I ran nearly all the way and my father and Humf will be here in a sec."

Elsie wiped her face with her apron and looked down at the eager girl whose cheeks were wet with tears.

"I know you're sorry, love. I asked your father not

to leave me alone and go off with that young chap. Too bad it is when your mother is taking a few hours off and enjoying a meal that somebody else has cooked . . . No, Lucy. I never seen the chap before but you know what your dad's like, and afore I knew what was happening he was whispering away to him at the corner table and then off they go together just as if it was closing time . . . Here he is now and you can help him in here and keep Humf out of the way."

Mr. Brown bustled into the kitchen and as Elsie passed him Lucy was astonished to hear him say, "Business looking up, Elsie! Just take their orders and I'll help in here. We must show Mrs. Brown that we can get on without her, mustn't we?"

"There's poached eggs on welsh rarebit for two and the other wants corned beef salad and the tin opener isn't where I left it, and when I've got the time Mr. Brown I'd like a private talk with you."

These remarks were made in a piercing whisper and Lucy sent up a silent prayer that the three customers hadn't heard her.

Humf took one look at his father and sister and disappeared upstairs. He was in no mood to discuss his future career, and although he was hungry he knew the others wouldn't allow him to eat in the café. So Lucy, not for the first time realised that she must try to keep the peace between her father and Elsie. This wasn't very difficult because with one of his sudden changes of mood Mr. Brown settled down to help. First he apologised to Elsie for leaving her so long, but explained that he had only done so because she was efficient and customers liked her much better than they liked him. He said nothing about the strange young man, but took off his coat and rolled up his sleeves and poached the eggs and found the tin opener. He refused to notice that Lucy was still a little sulky and told her that he had all sorts of plans for their holidays after they came back from Conways, but he didn't mention her mother's birthday, or why he was talking so secretly to a stranger in the grounds of the castle. So she said nothing about her mother either.

When the customers had been served, Mervyn sent Lucy upstairs with ices for Humf and herself and promised to call them for their dinner when the café was empty. They often did this in the holidays and Elsie joined them.

Soon after they had finished their meal, Mrs. Brown arrived laden with parcels and a large shopping bag. She was small and slim and fair like Lucy, who could never remember a time when her mother wasn't there when she was wanted. She was old enough to know that their father needed just as much looking after as Humf and herself, and although she couldn't have explained in words, she knew that Mary Brown with her unselfish love for them all made them into a wonderful family. She had bought them all, including Elsie, little presents from Brighton—a paperback story for Lucy, sweets for Humf, an egg-timer for the kitchen Elsie would have one day, and a new ballpoint pen for her husband who had a passion for writing materials and notebooks.

Nobody mentioned Mervyn's strange behaviour, but try as she would Lucy could not at first forget the way in which the unpleasant young man took off his dark specs and stared at them. There was something she didn't like about him, and the way in which he had taken some small article from his pocket was secretive. True, she had not seen her father take money from his pocket, but he might have done so while they had been hurrying down the steps.

Lucy never had secrets from her mother, but now that she was back home again with them she hated the idea of telling her what they had seen because she was sure it would worry her after a happy day.

Later, when they had closed the *Blackbirds*, Mervyn suggested that they should all stroll up the hill towards the downs to watch the sunset, and it was then that Humf changed his mind and told his parents about Dandy and his own ambitions.

"Excellent, my boy!" his father agreed. "Nothing like making up your mind about a career at an early age, but you mustn't get too set in your ways or in your ideas. That's a mistake which I've never made. I agree that there's not room in our present home for a large dog but I have some ambitious plans for the future."

Lucy and her mother exchanged a glance of dismay, but Humf was so surprised that he launched into a confused description of the cream and blue panda police cars, and how if he couldn't have a dog to train he'd like to have driving lessons as soon as possible. And so they came happily home as the last rays of the sinking sun touched the flint walls of the castle and brought a richer glow to the old red roofs of Malling.

It was very hot in Lucy's little room at the top of the house as she tossed and turned under a single sheet waiting for sleep that wouldn't come. Long after her mother had come up to kiss her there was another step on the stair and she heard her father whisper:

"Still awake, Lucy?"

"Yes, Dad. It's too hot. Come in and put on the light for me. I'll start the book Mum brought me."

He came in quietly and sat on the end of her bed. "Too late to read, my dear. Something I wanted to tell you. The man in the castle grounds today was talking business. Private business about your mother's birthday on Saturday. We've got to do something special about that, haven't we? Keep it a secret, Lucy love, and tell Humf not to tell your mother either . . . Promise me, Lucy."

He kissed her and she promised, but the church clock struck eleven times before she fell into a troubled sleep at last.

2

Wednesday: Deadman's Wood

CONWAYS was a big farm about three miles to the south of Malling. The house, which was built of the flints which for many hundreds of years have been dug by Sussex men from the chalk downs, was roofed with the rich, red tiles typical of the county. It stood on gently rising ground with a garden surrounded by a flint wall and guarded by a line of mighty beeches planted by Mr. Hogben's ancestors to break up the force of the gales that roared in from the sea during the winter months. The farmyard was on the left of the house with big barns on three sides of the square. Behind the house, facing a pleasant slope of pasture, were the stables where the farmer kept his precious hunters which were now mostly exercised by John and Peggy.

On the morning after which Lucy and Humf had seen their father with the mysterious stranger, John woke soon after six. He knew that his father would already be supervising the milking, but as this was the first full day of the holidays, and as the young Browns would not be over for some hours, there was time for him to ride before breakfast. Peggy wouldn't thank him to be wakened so early, so he washed and dressed quickly in jeans and an old khaki shirt. His mother—

short and plump and with a rosy face and her dark hair parted in the centre—was already in the kitchen. This room was the centre of the house and the centre of all their lives. It was big and friendly, and for as long as John could remember it had smelled of warm cooking and faintly of tobacco and herbs. The low ceiling was crossed with black beams which his father had told him were ships' timbers of Sussex oak hewn hundreds of years ago from the forests of the Weald. From these beams hung rows of pewter mugs and tankards and measures of gleaming copper, and in the centre of the longest wall was a fireplace like a small cave with a wooden bench on each side big enough for two to sit close together and watch the flames of a log fire on a winter's night. Indeed, many of John's earliest memories were of sitting here with his sister while their father told them tales of Sussex smugglers and the sons of Sussex Hogbens who had gone out of this old house in olden days to fight the French.

"Hullo, son," his mother smiled. "Going to give Sultan a run? Your dad is out there somewhere, but don't be too long. I want a word with you and Peggy about those Brown children before they arrive, and your father will want his breakfast in an hour."

John was as tall as his mother and gave her a quick hug as he went out into the farmyard and across to the stables of the two Hogben hunters which were his father's pride and joy although he was now too heavy to ride them much. The black was called Sultan and last spring, soon after the Browns had arrived in Malling, John had ridden him into second place in his first Point-to-Point race and this was still the most important day in his life. The chestnut with a white star on her forehead was Fair Lady and Peggy usually rode her.

Black Sultan whinnied a welcome as John saddled

him and five minutes later horse and boy were riding up the chalky lane. Before long Conways looked like a toy model far below. As the track levelled out, John checked the eager horse and looked down on the land that would be his one day. Apart from the fields into which the cattle were now wandering from the milking sheds, the broad acres of Conways were already glowing gold in the morning sun and John knew that next week the combine harvester would be working for perhaps eighteen hours a day if the weather held. Then he turned his eyes to the south where a clump of beech trees broke the smooth line of the downs and from which is was possible to see the sea. A lark rose a few feet away. The horse was impatient so John let him have his way. Suddenly the wind was whistling through his hair and there was only the thrill of horse and boy in motion together and the glorious solitude of the morning. Under the beeches John dismounted. Above him the sky was hidden under a soft curtain of green and beneath his feet crackled the crisp brown leaves of last autumn. Sultan knew this place well and walked patiently beside his young master. Just beyond the shadow of the trees was the ring of an ancient earthwork dug as a fortress by the vanished men of an age when the forests, which covered the land below the hills, were the home of wild beasts. The only weapons with which the warriors of these ancient people could protect their women and children and provide themselves with meat and clothing, were arrow and spear heads fashioned from the flint dug from the chalk. John and Peggy had often found some of these.

Sultan stood for him to mount and then cantered across the short turf to where the great chalk cliffs fell sharply to the sea. A few fishing boats were coming in with the tide to Newhaven and overhead the gulls sailed effortlessly. It was good to remember that there was no school for weeks, and perhaps it would be fun to teach Lucy and young Humf how to camp out and have fun in the country.

By the time he had rubbed down Sultan, breakfast was ready. Mrs. Hogben didn't believe in a farmer starting the day with a piece of toast and a cup of coffee. He had always been a big man with a voice and a hearty manner to match a splendid bushy moustache. When he had emptied his third large cup of tea he sat back and beamed at his family.

"Next Monday I reckon, if the weather holds," he said, and they all knew what he meant. "Make the best of this week with the young Browns and give 'em a good time. Nice kids. Your mother says you want to take 'em camping, but she's something to say to you about them. Out with it, Mother."

"It's about Humf," Mrs. Hogben said. "I reckon you two think he's too young to do everything you want to do, but he's a plucky one and I want you to give him and Lucy a good time. It's their mother who worries me. She's working too hard without enough help. I've been into the café once or twice lately. They've made a nice place of the *Blackbirds*, and your father agrees that it will give Mrs. Brown a break for a few days if those two were here. We telephoned Pollards last week and the Strangs say you can camp out in their field that runs down to Deadman's Wood. You can do no harm there if you're careful about your fire. The Browns won't have done anything like that afore . . . I'll take Peggy into Malling in the car right away and we'll pick up Lucy and Humf and have a chat with Mrs. Brown before they get too busy. John can pack up the tent and sleeping bags and all your gear while we're away, and then one of us will ring up the Strangs and see if we can bring you all over after dinner."

"No argy-bargy about those arrangements," Mr. Hogben smiled as he got up. "What your mother says goes in this house, and I'll phone Strang."

Ten minutes later Peggy and her mother were on their way in to Malling in the farmer's estate car. As they turned into Pottery Lane they saw a police panda in its smart pale blue livery with white doors and white strip across the roof. It was outside the *Blackbirds*, and Humf was standing on one leg with excitement talking to the driver.

As Mrs. Hogben drew up behind it she remarked, as most people do when they see the police doing something to help somebody else, "What's wrong now, Peg? Doesn't look as if there's been an accident. Stay here until I see what's to do."

As Humf recognised her, he ran up to greet them. "Hullo," he gasped. "Sorry if we're not quite ready but we got important visitors. We got two policemen and one's inside with Mum and this one who drives this smashing panda is called Robert and he says one day p'raps, if I can really help, he'll take me a drive and I can flash the blue light . . . Come and say 'Hullo' to him, Peggy. He's a super man. Lucy's upstairs and Dad's gone what he calls marketing and the other panda man is talking to Mum. He's this panda man's mate and they go everywhere together and they've got radio but they haven't got a dog."

"I should think not indeed," Mrs. Hogben said as she got out and smiled at the driver who seemed highly amused by Humf and invited him to come and sit next to him until his mate was ready.

Humf didn't need a second invitation and was in the car before Peggy had followed her mother into the café. Mrs. Brown, looking pale and tired, was sitting opposite the other constable whose cap was on the table between them. Both of them were smiling and the man got up as the farmer's wife stepped forward.

"I'm sorry the children aren't ready yet," Mrs. Brown apologised. "This, Constable Harris, is Mrs. Hogben of Conways Farm, and if you haven't done so already, you'd better tell her what you've just told me and save yourself a journey. And if it's not too soon after breakfast I'll make us all some coffee. What's happened to my son?"

"He's going to drive the panda any minute now," Peggy said. "If what you're talking about is private would you like me to go up and help Lucy?"

The constable looked at her mother. "She might as well hear what we've got to tell you. We'll be calling at most of the farms today, and thanks all the same Mrs. Brown, but we don't often take refreshment on duty. What I have to say won't take long."

Peggy wished John had been there to hear how the constable told his story.

"We'd like to have a talk with a woman with short grey hair who's been seen in these parts lately. She's an artist and calls at farmhouses and some of the big houses which look as if they'd make a good picture, and offers to paint them and sell them to the owner. Tramps about the country with her gear in a rucksack—little stool and all—and does her pictures and asks plenty of questions and likes to have a look over the house if she can. Would you have seen a woman like that round Conways, Mrs. Hogben?"

"If I had I'd reckon she was stark staring crazy. We've got no time to spare for the likes of silly women unless she'd like to paint the doors and window frames of the house that should have been done years ago. Who wants pictures of the place they live in anyway? And if I may make so bold as to ask, young man, why are you spending your time going round in a smart car at harvest when my man has hardly got time to eat . . ."

She paused for breath and then pointed dramatically at the startled Mrs. Brown.

"And another thing, what's all this nonsense got to do with my friend Mrs. Brown who's got no time to waste either? And what with all these smart cars and your radio talk, talk to each other and 'Z Cars' on the telly, it seems funny to me that you can't find a crazy woman who only wants to sit down and paint pictures that nobody wants to buy . . . What did you say your name was, young man?"

"I didn't say, madam," the young man answered without much enthusiasm. "You haven't given me a chance but Mrs. Brown was good enough to introduce me. I'm Police Constable Harris and I'm trying to do my duty. Some of the houses at which the woman calls are subsequently broken into and we have received complaints that articles of value have been taken. In many such instances, the woman has been invited into the house to take refreshment, and as it is my duty to protect the public we are trying to warn the occupants of all isolated houses. Should any such woman ask to sketch your house or even to look over it, madam, we ask you to telephone us immediately."

Mrs. Hogben sat down and roared with laughter.

"Well said, Constable Bill Harris. I remember your mother before you were born and I'll remember what you say now. And what's all this to do with my friend Mrs. Brown? I hope you're not bothering her about filling up papers and the like just because she's making the *Blackbirds* a worthwhile place in Malling?"

Mrs. Brown laughed.

"The constable has been very kind, Mrs. Hogben, and so have you. All that he's doing is to ask all the café and restaurant owners to keep a lookout for this woman . . . She might even ask us to show some of her pictures and try to sell them for her. I'll ask my husband and Elsie who helps us to keep a lookout for a grey-haired artist, and although we haven't got a telephone yet, we'll let you know quickly if the woman comes in here . . . This must be very difficult for you because there always seem to be plenty of artists sketching the castle and streets of Malling . . . Run along up and find Lucy, Peggy. Maybe she doesn't know what clothes to take and you can help her. I'll get Humf along in a minute and I know we mustn't keep your mother waiting. It's kind of her to call for you."

"It's me, Lucy," Peggy called out at the foot of the narrow stairs which led up to the two little rooms under the eaves where the Brown children slept. "I've come to help you pack because Mum's brought me in the car and she's in a hurry. Did you know you've got two smashing policemen in a panda car downstairs?"

"Policemen?" Lucy gasped as she came out on the landing. "What for? Where's Dad? What do they want?"

Peggy came and sat on the end of her bed and told her how few clothes she would need to bring and that she thought their parents would rather they camped near the forest than at the sea and that they were fixing everything with their friends at Pollards.

"But bring your swim suit all the same. Maybe we'll get a chance at Greenhaven if the tide is right . . . What's wrong, Lucy? You O.K.? You want to come, don't you? Or are you fussing because Humf won't be able to keep up with us?"

"Of course I want to come. So does Humf and you and John are very decent about him. I know he's only a kid but he does try to do things with us without spoiling everything. Why are these policemen downstairs? Humf was telling me about one who came with a dog to his school the other day. Humf is crazy about being a dog handler now. What do these men want here? I s'pose Dad has done something wrong or silly."

Lucy told her about the grey-haired artist and things being stolen from farms and lonely houses and that the police were on the lookout for suspicious strangers. "That's why they're asking Mrs. Brown and other café keepers to keep a lookout as well. Your dad isn't there anyway."

"But that's ridiculous," Lucy said. "Nearly everybody who comes into the café is a stranger so how should we know? When Dad comes back I hope Mum won't tell him. I must warn Humf not to tell him either. Dad will think everybody who comes in is a suspicious artist and make all sorts of trouble. You don't know what he's like sometimes, Peggy."

"Maybe I don't, but I like him. He makes me laugh. You're worried about him aren't you, Lucy? You don't have to tell me anything you don't want to, but it's just as well that we don't all have the same sort of parents, isn't it? Mum says your mother works too hard and isn't well. D'you want to tell me all about it? Are you really worried? My mum likes you a lot."

Lucy would have liked to have told Peggy about her father and the strange man she had seen showing him something in the castle grounds yesterday. She could not forget this unpleasant looking stranger, nor the way in which her father had come up here to her last night, and without actually asking her not to mention to their mother what she and Humf had seen, making it clear enough that it was a secret that belonged to the three of them. Lucy knew that her father would not lie to her but she was also sure that he might well have done something which would worry her mother. And now, much as she wanted to go off with Peggy and

John, she hated having this sort of secret from her mother. But she didn't think she could find the courage to ask her father about the mysterious stranger before they left. She wondered too, what he would say if her mother told him about the policeman's visit, which she was almost certain to do. She also wished Mark was coming with them today. She could tell him all about it more easily than the Hogbens. She knew he would be sensible and help her. He was John and Peggy's friend too, but he was the sort of boy who would keep somebody else's secret, but after what he had said yesterday she didn't want to bother him.

So all she said was, "I am fussed about my mother, Peggy. I know she works too hard, and although our Dad gets the most wonderful ideas, and although Elsie is marvellous, somehow it's always Mum who has to do the worrying . . . Let's go now. We've never been camping before, so you won't think we're too soppy about it if we make mistakes will you?"

Peggy didn't say much but every time she met Lucy she liked her more. For the first time in her life she was beginning to understand what it must be like to be insecure about home and parents. She could not remember a time when she had been really worried about her father or mother. They had always been at Conways. The farm was her home and she had hardly ever left it. Hogbens had always lived there and Peggy was fairly sure that when she married she wouldn't want to go very far away either, but that was something that wouldn't happen for years and years. Now she realised that her new friends hadn't got much money, and that their mother was working too hard while their father didn't seem to be much help. Suddenly she determined to show Lucy that she did care about them all, and even if her new friend didn't want to tell her anything else now, perhaps if she was patient Lucy would trust her and tell her what was really worrying her.

"Come on then, Lucy. Let's hurry. We've got two tents and four sleeping bags at Conways and John is getting all that sort of thing together. Bring pyjamas and your washing things and if we do go to Pollards Mrs. Strang lets us wash in her bathroom. There's no water down where we camp and we have to carry it from the house. We'll show you how to make a fire and cook our meals, but we must be very careful about the fire because of the forest. You'll like Mr. and Mrs. Strang although Dad doesn't think he's much of a farmer. Maybe he's a bit like your dad because I'm sure he's done all sorts of other things, and I've never met anybody who can tell so many stories about what really happened—especially things in Sussex. He even knows more than our father. We'll ask him to come to our camp fire tonight and he'll talk and talk until we forget where we are."

Lucy didn't care for Peggy's remarks about her father "doing all sorts of things," because this was only too true, but she did say that their father knew lots of history too and read many books and talked to them about all sorts of fascinating things.

They were in Humf's room when the little boy came puffing up the stairs with the news that the two constables had gone and had promised him a ride in the panda one day.

"And Peggy's mother says please to get a move on because she's in a hurry now, and Mum says not to worry about her because Elsie has sent a message to say she'll be round in ten minutes and Dad hasn't come back . . . And thanks very much for coming into my private room and if you'll kindly take the luggage down I'd like to have a private look round just to see if I've got all I want for this exploration. What about my compass, f'rinstance? The compass my dad bought me at that stall in the market one day. Everybody wants a compass in a forest. And my torch that flashes green and red if it's got a battery. Girls don't think of these things so please go away."

They went, and Humf soon followed them without admitting that he'd forgotten he'd swapped the compass for a knife, which he had now lost, and hadn't enough money for a battery. Mrs. Hogben was already in the car and neither Elsie nor Mr. Brown had arrived so there wasn't much time for prolonged farewells.

"Don't go wandering off on your own, Humf," Mrs. Brown pleaded. "We know that you're a keen explorer, but I rely on you to look after him, Lucy . . . And love, don't forget to telephone Mrs. Robson at the greengrocer's down the street if you want us. You know how kind she is, and Mrs. Hogben has given us the Pollards Farm number so we shall be in touch . . . Goodbye, darlings. I shall be all right. Have a lovely time and I'll see you on Friday night or Saturday."

She came out on to the pavement to see them off and, as usual, Lucy hated saying goodbye to her. And as Mrs. Hogben drove them back to Conways Lucy began to think about the three people whom the police had told about the grey-haired artist—her mother, Mrs. Hogben and Peggy. How much Humf knew she wasn't yet sure, and how much her mother would tell Mervyn and Elsie she didn't know either.

By the time they were back at the farm, John had packed nearly everything and told them that the Strangs would be pleased to see them this afternoon and that they were welcome to camp in their field.

"Dad's off somewhere in the Land-Rover," he went on, "but he'll take us over after dinner. Mr. Strang wants advice about something. Come and see the horses, Lucy. We'll put you up on Fair Lady if you like. No more excuses. She's as gentle as a baby."

Lucy's first ride wasn't such a terrible ordeal, and what surprised her most was the distance she was from the ground! Peggy showed her how to sit, how to hold the mare's reins, how to try to move with her and above all else, how to inspire the horse with confidence and not to show her own fear.

"Well done, little Lucy," John teased as he helped her to dismount. "We'll have you up every time you come to Conways if you go on like this. What about you, Humf?"

"It's dogs I like, thanks all the same, John. I 'preciate you asking me but I don't even mind big dogs. Has Mr. Strang got a dog?"

Peggy explained that the Strangs had a bitch called Jess who was going to have puppies soon, and that they would probably train one of these for Conways because theirs was getting very old.

At dinner time Mrs. Hogben told her husband about the police warning of the woman artist, and Humf took the opportunity of explaining about Dandy and his ambitions.

"I've heard tell of these dogs," the farmer agreed. "Strang will know more about 'em than I do because the police often train 'em in the forest. As for all this talk of crazy women artists I reckon it's a lot of nonsense. There's always somebody about a farm and not many of us have got anything worth pinching. What the police ought to be doing round here is keeping idle folk in cars off my land and leaving gates open and chucking down their broken bottles and lighting fires. And when they've done all that I'd be obliged if they'd find me a place in Malling where I can park my car on market days!"

He seemed to think the last comment was a huge joke and roared with laughter as he cut himself a second hunk of cheese. All except Humf laughed dutifully with him, but he had a more important question.

"This place where we're going to camp I want to ask about, please. John says it's called Deadman's Wood. Are there dead men in it now? What's in it? Wolves and snakes?"

John realised that he was serious.

"No wolves, Humf, but there are adders and we have to be careful not to tread on them. They're not big—about one and a half feet long and you can tell them because they've got a black zig-zag mark all down their backs. They like the sunshine and a warm bank or stone but they won't hurt you if you don't disturb them. We'll ask Mr. Strang to tell you about Deadman's Wood. It's part of a big forest you'll see this afternoon and it's called that because three smugglers who came ashore at Greenhaven were chased into it by the redcoats who were always trying to catch them."

"I bet Dandy would have caught them," Humf announced with relish. "Is it called Deadman's Wood 'cos they were killed there by the soldiers? Is it haunted by smuggling ghosts?"

"Don't be ridiculous, Humf," Lucy said in a smug, elder-sister sort of way. "Of course there aren't any ghosts and anyway it all happened a long time ago and criminals and soldiers too were always getting killed in those days."

The State Forest of which Deadman's Wood was a small part, stretched for some miles along the northern side of the coast road. It was divided, in case of fire which is the foresters greatest danger, by wide grassy "rides," but apart from these wide spaces there were very few footpaths between the orderly rows of conifers and young beech trees. In some places the forest was a mile deep and on its northern edge the notorious and much older Deadman's Wood grew densely round a shallow chalk pit on the Strangs' land.

It was a long way round by road from Conways to Pollards, and when Mr. Hogben drew up in front of the old house and sounded his horn, Lucy and Humf realised that this isolated place was different from the cheerful, bustling Conways. Pollards was certainly very old and partly overshadowed by huge beech trees and although the walls were undoubtedly of flint the front of the low house was covered with the biggest mass of white roses the children had ever seen. Pollards was more of a large cottage than a farmhouse, and they discovered later that Mr. Strang was mostly engaged in raising turkeys and rented many of his pastures to other farmers at certain times of the year for fattening their stock.

As John helped Humf to jump out of the Land-Rover, Mr. Strang came out of the house followed by a black and white bitch large with an unborn litter.

Peggy had tried to explain that Mr. Strang didn't look a farmer, but the Browns were nevertheless surprised to see that although he was nearly bald he wore a neat little beard and dark rimmed spectacles. He shook hands with Mr. Hogben, said "Hullo" to John and Peggy and then turned to welcome Lucy and Humf both of whom were feeling shy.

"We're glad to have you here. Peggy and John will show you where to pitch your tents. You may have a fire for cooking but none of you are to leave it burning. And you must carry down your own water supply and have a bucketful ready to douse the fire if the wind is strong enough to make the sparks fly. Now here's Mrs. Strang, who thinks anybody who prefers to sleep out of doors rather than in a bed must be mad, so we'll leave the back door unlatched in case any of you want to come into the house in the night. That way you can do so without waking us up. Not you of course, young man. Anyone can see that you're a born camper, but I may as well warn you that there's thunder about and we could have a storm tonight . . . Now be off with you and I'll come and inspect your camp presently."

Mrs. Strang proved to be a woman of very few words. She was as neat and tidy as her house, which she insisted on showing Lucy and Humf before they ran down the field to inspect the camping site. The living room of Pollards was lined with books, and when Lucy asked if she might look at one about Malling which was illustrated with old prints, Mrs. Strang sat down at the table with her and showed her a picture of Pottery Lane as it looked nearly a century ago.

So Lucy told her about the *Blackbirds* and how kind the Hogbens had been and that Mark Simson was teaching her about birds, and neither of them noticed that Humf had wandered out into the sunshine and was making a fuss of Jess.

Lucy liked Mrs. Strang at once. It was difficult to guess her age because, although her hair was white, her face was without wrinkles and her eyes very blue. Unlike the jolly Mrs. Hogben, she spoke quietly, rarely laughed but had a very sweet smile.

"Remember what my husband said, Lucinda, and don't forget to come into the house in the night if you want to. I shall call you Lucinda because it's a pretty name and it suits you, and I shall come and see your mother when I am next in town. We don't go out much and the winters are rather long. It seems an age since Mr. Strang was a teacher, but the doctor's told him that he must live in the country, and so here we are and very blessed in many ways. If you like books and pictures and beautiful things, my dear, you must come here as often as you can. My George will have plenty to tell you, and if you like music you can listen to our record player with us . . . And now there's Mr. Hogben sounding his horn. That means he wants to be off. We'll go and say 'Goodbye' to him."

"Not to worry, Lucy," he shouted above the roar of the engine. "We'll telephone Win Robson and ask her to tell your mother you've arrived safely, had your first ride on a horse's back, and that your Humf is still behaving himself. You can use Mr. Strang's 'phone any time, and we'll come and fetch you back to Conways if the weather breaks . . . Cheerio, all," and he drove off as if he hadn't a minute to spare.

Mr. Strang walked down the field with Lucy and Humf to where the others were already putting up the two tents. The camp was well set in the little hollow about two hundred yards from where the dark ranks of the forest trees halted their march at a fence of wire netting which was to guard the young trees from rabbits.

"Can we go into Deadman's Wood?" Humf asked Mr. Strang. "I can see a gate. And what about the wild beasts and the adders? Do the snakes come out here?"

"No they don't, Humphrey, and you can walk on any of the forest paths and rides as long as you never light a fire, or cut any of the live trees or interfere with any of the water tanks which are kept full in different parts of the forest in case there is a fire. And you mustn't leave any glass bottles there because the sun shining through broken glass could start a fire. The men we know who look after the forest are called foresters and some of them kill adders when they see them and hang them up on the wire fence or a gate just to warn people to be careful. But don't you worry.

Adders only come out on the sunny places and they won't bite unless you tread on them or frighten them. If you see one wriggling across a rock or in the grass stand still and let him go."

"And you may as well know what to do if one of us gets bitten," John said tersely. "Tie a handkerchief or a bit of string or a tie or something as tight as you can above the bite so that the poison won't reach the heart. Then cut the bite and suck out the blood and the poison."

"And then get the patient to a hospital where they'll give you an anti-something injection," Peggy added cheerfully. "And don't look so disgusted, Lucy, 'cos this is what living in the country means, and you're much more likely to be knocked down by a 'bus or a car in Malling than you are to be bitten by an adder here . . . Now see how we build a fire in between these bricks. If the wind is blowing from the east or north, we're not allowed to light the fire because sparks might blow into the forest, but we'll be okay today shan't we, Mr. Strang? Good! And what we want now is tea, so fill that old kettle from the pail, Lucy, and then help me unpack the mugs. We've got enough twigs and dry wood to start the fire, but Humf had better make it his job to keep us supplied with fuel. Plenty of dead wood under the trees, Humf, so off you go. There's an old sack here somewhere, so you can fill that and we'll keep the fire going gently until supper time."

Humf didn't care for Peggy in this bossy mood, but as Mr. Strang offered to come with him a little way into the wood he decided that it was better not to squabble and went quietly enough, and soon found himself chatting naturally to one of the nicest men he had ever known.

On the wooden post of the gate into the forest were nailed the limp, mutilated bodies of five small adders.

"Just to remind you what they look like," Mr. Strang explained as he opened the gate. "Some gamekeepers hang up the dead bodies of stoats and jays that eat the eggs of pheasants. Our foresters don't like adders but I can't really see the sense of doing this . . . Don't be afraid of living things, my boy. Come here as often as you like and learn to know the forest. Next time you come into the forest I'll take you and the others for a long walk—maybe tomorrow if I've the time—and we'll never see another living person. Listen and all you can hear is the traffic on the coast road . . . It's good to be quiet sometimes, Humphrey. The world is much too noisy and trees grow without making any noise . . . I'm going back now and I'll tell the others you won't be long. Don't go too far from the path, and fill your sack with twigs and fir cones. Good luck. Just pretend you're an explorer blazing a trail . . . Come up to the house when you want to, but I've got to take Mrs. Strang out in the car for an hour soon."

Humf stood still until his new friend had disappeared and realised how quietly he moved. From far away he heard the voices of the others in the camp and then crawled under the trees and filled his sack. He found his way back past the adders without any worry, but when he tried to explain how enormous were the serpents he had killed single-handed and how the trackless forest was infested with wild beasts, they told him to run up to the house for more water. And when he had struggled back with a pail much too heavy for him John sent him back for matches, and so it went on until, in a furious temper, Humf snatched up the sack and shouted:

"You can all jolly well roast yourselves to a frizzle with your stupid fire and wear yourselves out getting things for yourselves. I'm fed up with you and I'm going to make my own camp. I'm not your blooming slave and I hope you're all haunted by dead smugglers and adders."

An hour later when the first peal of thunder rumbled round the hills, Lucy realised that her brother was not with them. Neither Peggy nor John had seen him and the latter suggested that he had got bored and gone back to the house.

This remark annoyed Lucy.

"You've no right to say that, John, and I don't think you're funny. Just because Humf is the youngest you've kept him running errands and dashing about and picking up sticks like those kids in Grimm's Fairy Tales . . . And if you haven't heard of those ask Peggy. She's young enough to remember fairy tales," and with this outburst she ran up the field towards the house.

The camp, in its hollow, was soon out of sight, and the only sound was the rather ridiculous cooing of wood pigeons and the distant hum of traffic. After a few visits to Conways, Lucy was getting used to the sights and smells of the country, but Pollards was much quieter and more remote than the Hogbens place, busy with the hum of the milking machines and the throb of tractors. When she was near enough to the house to be heard, she paused to regain her breath and then shouted for Humf. There was no reply so she decided to run round to the back of the house to ask Mrs. Strang if she had seen him. She called his name and as she crossed the yard she noticed that the back door was ajar. Months ago she had learned that farmers were careless about locking up, but as she pushed back the door and stepped into the stone-flagged kitchen she wondered why the dog hadn't barked a warning. Suddenly she was scared. She called again in a strained, breathless voice, "Mrs. Strang? Are you upstairs? We've lost Humf. Have you seen him?"

No answer. No sound but that of a dripping tap. She was alone in a strange, empty house where no watchdog barked and no friendly voice answered. Her heart thumped with sudden fear as she stepped on tiptoe to another half-open door at the foot of the stairs. She opened her mouth to call again, but no sound came from her lips as she heard the sound of a step behind her.

She turned and her hand flew to her face. A man was watching her through the kitchen window. His reddish hair was unkempt and he was wearing dark specs. For a long moment they stared at each other and then, as if he had recognised her, he turned away.

3

Wednesday: Alone in the Forest

BY NATURE, HUMF was a good-humoured little boy. He was used to being the youngest of his family and knew how best to get along with his difficult father. He loved his mother, and although Lucy sometimes tried to order him about, the brother and sister were very good friends. But the move to Malling, the new school, and Lucy's friendship for Mark and the Hogbens had not made life easier for Humf. Both John and Mark were good enough to him when they remembered, but nothing could alter the difference in the years between them. Also Humf, so far, had not made any real friends of his own age.

Mark was fun and told him about the country and didn't complain much when he wanted to come along with Lucy and the others to watch birds and visit their secret camp at Galleybird Pit. John, who rode the great Black Sultan like a real jockey, and was Humf's hero, was decent enough to him when he noticed him, but it is never easy for the youngest of a group of friends to realise without being told when they are in the way.

Mr. Strang, with his quiet voice and kindly eyes had been good to them, and had not even suggested that a small boy who he had only just met might even be afraid of a dead adder. And this nice man had not spoken to him as if he was only nine.

At first, Humf had not much minded being sent to gather sticks and fetch water which slopped over his sandalled feet. But when John, busy and bossy about knocking in tent pegs and showing off to Lucy, had told Humf just now to keep out of the way and fetch more wood, something frightening had happend to him. It wasn't just being spoken to like this before the others that brought tears of shame and fury to his eyes. That had happened before. It was not even that John was showing off a little because after all he was the eldest and the cleverest of them all. Neither was Humf very concerned that Lucy and Peggy seemed to have forgotten him. The awful thing was that when he shouted that he wasn't their slave, John had just looked up and laughed at him. It was then that Humf became a different person. The horrid words he wanted to say choked in his throat, and his head throbbed, and there was a red mist before his eyes as he ran blindly from them and down the field and through the gate where the dead adders were hanging.

He ran up the path along which Mr. Strang had recently led him. He ran, with faltering steps and thudding heart while thunder rolled round the hills and the sky darkened above the tree tops. He ran without knowing where he was going, and when his weary legs collapsed under him he did not at first realise that he had fallen at the junction of the path that led from Pollards with one of the great grassy roads that ran, straight as rulers, through the forest. For a few minutes he lay with his face on the turf which was always kept cut short so that fire, fanned by the wind, would not spread across it. Slowly his breathing became normal, and as he opened his eyes he was aware of a strange, sweet smell. His face was pressed against a clump of tiny mauve flowers. It was many weeks later, when Humf knew her better, that Mrs. Strang showed him a picture of these flowers in an old book, and told him that they were a herb called wild thyme which flourished on chalky soil. He never forgot the evening when he first realised how smells often remind us of something that happened to us, more than what we see.

After a little he sat up. He was alone in a strange new world. Behind him the green ride ran steeply up between the stiff ranks of the trees and the chalky banks were gay with purple scabious. The sun was hidden behind dark thunder clouds, no bird sang, no leaf rustled and as Humf slowly stood up he knew that he was lost. He looked down at the sun-baked soil, wondering whether he would see the quick flicker of an adder's zig-zag back. And what animals, he wondered, were watching him warily from the cover of the dark forest? How far had he run from the camp before he fell? Were the others searching for him now or did they even care about his fate? And even if he called, would they hear? John would probably still be telling the others how clever he was. And where was Pollards? And without sun or compass, how could he know whether he was walking south towards the main road where there would surely be somebody who would take him back to Malling? Perhaps even a panda car? Suddenly a jagged flash of lightning split the sky, but the following mutter of thunder was faint and far away.

Then he noticed that the narrow path up which he had fled from the scorn of the others continued in the same direction on the other side of the ride. Each looked alike and he could not now remember along which path he had fled. Perhaps if he took the track on his left he would soon recognise some flower, or unusual tree or chalky bank which he had passed when he was running away? He had also lost count of time, but as he stood, still feeling rather dizzy and struggling to remember, some of his courage returned. Somebody—probably his mother—had once told him that to lose your temper was to waste your time and that there were better ways of using time. By now he had almost forgotten the rage that had sent him off in hatred from the others. For a while at least he was no longer Humphrey Mervyn Brown but an explorer in a strange land.

"No use standing about here doing nothing," he said in a reasonably firm voice. "I'm not the first explorer to have lost his compass and missed the way back to the camp after being sore wounded. All I've got to do is to use my wits and go back the way I came. O' course we've got to look out for the man-eating serpents and the savages lurking in these trackless forests but that's easy enough if we just keep calm."

It was at this stage of his one-sided conversation that while keeping calm Humf took the wrong path, and instead of going back towards Pollards, continued into the depths of the forest in the opposite direction and passed nothing that he recognised. For ten minutes the explorer kept his head and his courage by discussing his prospects with himself, but when every turn in the path disclosed no fresh view and led only to another corner exactly like the last, some of his fears returned. Twice he stood still and listened, but no sound except that of his own breath broke the silence. Presently he came to another of the great rides and was not sure whether it was the one he must have left half an hour ago. Or was it an hour? The close ranks of the trees looked the same. The conifers—which to him were Christmas trees—were all carrying the same bluish-green unripe cones. The smaller beech trees crowded between them were bright with their leaves of a lighter green, but what he saw were thousands and thousands of silent trees standing like sentinels in dark ranks.

Once he jumped with fright as, with a harsh cry like a mocking laugh a bird with pinkish-brown plumage and black and white on its head and wings flew overhead. Mark had never shown him a jay, and this strange bird did nothing to make Humf feel any braver. He was sure now that he was the only human in this great deserted forest.

For a little while he lay again on the grass and rested, feeling strangely alone. Only once he thought about Lucy and the others and wondered if they were searching for him. Then he realised that he was thirsty and remembered a story, told him probably by his father, of lost explorers who, tormented by thirst, wandered in circles for days in the desert. Then the distant thunder rumbled again and a few heavy, hot drops of rain fell on his face. Reassured that he was unlikely to die of thirst, he turned over and watched a bee busy on the pink blossoms of clover a few inches away.

Then he thought again of John and Peggy and of Lucy who didn't care when they ordered him to run to and fro for wood and water, and wondered whether they really were looking for him.

He stood up and shouted.

"I'm Humf and I'm lost! I'm Humf in the forest!"

but all that happened was that a rather horrid black bird flapped slowly from the top branches of a tree. No friendly voice answered him.

Then he panicked. He ran up the ride, feeling sure that when he reached the top there would surely be something to see besides trees. Perhaps he would be be able to look down on that familiar green meadow and see Pollards? Perhaps he wasn't really far from those kindly people who didn't even know that John and Peggy had sent him off for about twenty miles to find more wood, on a hot day, for their silly fire?

So he trotted wearily up the hill and this time he imagined that he was the nice police officer in charge of that super dog Dandy. What would he do if Dandy was with him now? He had left Dandy's comic in a secret place in his room at home, but if he could be sure that the nice Sergeant Harry was somewhere in this forest with Dandy, they would soon find Pollards for him and make the others look silly. He hoped that Lucy was sorry for him. If she had any sense she would by now be making arrangements for panda cars to search for him. Trouble was that she might not have been listening properly when he had told her all about Dandy when they were in the castle. And this reminded him of the red-headed man they had seen showing something to their father. There was some sort of grown-up secret about that meeting which he did not like. As he had walked back to the *Blackbirds* yesterday, his father had asked him not to tell his mother because he had been talking with this man about a birthday surprise. But Humf wasn't sure that this was so. It was probably *nearly* true, or his father hoped it was true, which was almost the same thing. Lucy hadn't said anything to him about it either.

He was very tired when he reached four tall trees that were growing on the top of the rise up which he had been struggling. But this was not the top of the hill, and still there was nothing to see but the endless forest and a grey, lifeless sky. He looked up at the trees and was reminded of the four smugglers who had run for their lives through Deadman's Wood and had then been caught and perhaps hanged from these very branches.

And it was then that Humf forgot all about friendly policemen and being a brave explorer and became an exhausted, lonely and frightened little boy. He was confused and lost and even John, Peggy and Lucy who had deserted him would have been welcome. Half blinded with tears and knowing that he could go no further, he clutched at the trunk of the nearest tree. He was wearing sandals and no socks and as he trod on something slippery his foot turned over and with a sharp, searing pain in his ankle he fell to the ground.

He bent forward and with a cry of pain clutched his injured foot and saw blood oozing between his fingers. The pain stabbed up his bare leg and his last thought, before he fainted with shock, was that he had been bitten by an adder.

Then from far, far away he heard the barking of a dog. He struggled back to consciousness and felt the pain in his foot. When he opened his eyes, he saw standing over him, a great dog with a lolling tongue which lifted its head to bark and bark again.

"It's Dandy," Humf whispered. "Good dog, Dandy!" and as the dog lowered his head to lick his face the little boy put his arms round his neck and clung to him with all his strength.

4

Wednesday: The Search

It was only for a few seconds that Lucy and the red-haired man stared at each other through Mrs. Strang's kitchen window. The door into the yard was still open, the tap over the sink still dripped and Lucy's heart thumped with the shock. The stranger's hand moved to his face to remove his sun specs and then, as if he recognised her, he turned away and she heard his foot-steps cross the yard. Surely the man could not be a stranger to the Strangs else the bitch would have barked? Then Lucy remembered that the dog had not given warning of her either. Had the man heard her coming and hidden until she had entered the house? She remembered now that somebody had said that the Strangs were going out for about an hour. Was it Humf? Was she fussing about nothing and had her brother just run off in a temper to the house some other way and been given a lift by Mr. and Mrs. Strang? But surely the only way from Deadman's Wood back to Pollards was by the gate through which she had seen him run into the forest? And would he not have to pass the camp to get back to the house? As she considered this she knew that the three of them had behaved badly to him. She was sure, too, that the man who had watched her through the window just now was the stranger to whom her father was talking secretly in the castle grounds yesterday. But what was the man doing here, and could she now be sure that this house really was empty? And suppose she went out to call the others, would the stranger be hiding in the yard waiting for her because he recognised her from yesterday's brief encounter? She had not heard the sound of a car and there was still the mystery of the watch dog that didn't bark.

Surely the Strangs would not mind if she went upstairs to make sure the house was empty? She listened carefully again. Only the dripping tap and the distant mutter of thunder. At the foot of the stairs she called Mrs. Strang's name. Then:

"Humf! Are you hiding from us? Don't be silly if you are. We want you, Humf, and John is sorry about asking you to get all that wood. We're ready to cook now and I've come to fetch you."

No answer. Bravely she walked up the stairs. The doors of two bedrooms and the bathroom were open and there was no doubt that the house was empty. From a little open window on the landing she could smell the roses which would always remind her of Pollards. She stood on tiptoe and leaned out. She could see down the slope of the field to where their camp was hidden in its hollow and the rampart of the forest beyond. There was something almost sinister about those dark ranks of silent trees. Lucy had never before thought of trees in this way. They were alive and growing, and until the wind stirred them into movement they were so *quiet*. Today, now, everything was silent and still and waiting for a storm—everything, that is, except the swifts flashing and swooping round the house uttering their weird, high-pitched cries. Somebody had once told her that from earliest times, man had considered swifts to be birds of ill-omen.

Lucy wondered if John and Peggy would hear if she shouted for them, but then decided not to show them that she was frightened. Again she wished that Mark was here because she didn't really want to tell the Hogbens about the red-headed man she had seen with her father yesterday. She knew that neither of them could understand him as Mark did. He was so different from the Hogbens' bluff, down-to-earth father, and what was so particularly difficult was trying to explain to their friends that Mervyn didn't always mean exactly what he said. Humf and she—and their mother more than either of them—knew that he sometimes believed that something was going to happen just because he wanted it to do so. Mervyn had always wanted the best for all of them, and the only time he was really downhearted was when his hopes were not fulfilled. Lucy had once tried to explain this to Mark and to her surprise he had understood, but she was sure that although John and Peggy liked her father, and were often amused by him, they thought he was a failure who made his wife work too hard.

All these thoughts bothered her as she stood at the landing window of Pollards and watched the swifts swoop across the darkening sky. There was no doubt now that the house was empty. Humf had disappeared and John and Peggy must help her at once to look for him. She knew how upset he had been, and surely it would be possible to get lost in the forest? It could be that Humf was deliberately hiding to scare them, but he was their responsibility and they must find him before the Strangs returned, so she decided to run back to John and Peggy.

The kitchen door into the yard was still ajar and the tap was still dripping. She moved quietly, and as her tidy mother would have done, she tightened the tap. And then she did two sensible things. She locked the front door from the inside, leaving the key in the lock, made certain that the windows of the sitting-room were latched and then locked the kitchen door from the outside and put the key in the pocket of her jeans. Although she tried hard to banish the thought that the stranger might be hiding close by and watching her, she kept up her courage with the thought that when they had seen each other through the window he had been the first to run away. So, for a few moments, she stood still, wondering where the man had been hiding when she ran into the yard to see if Humf was in the house. She stood where he had watched her through the kitchen window but was not tall enough to see clearly into the room. And then she wondered again whether he was a friend of the Strangs because the dog hadn't barked. Perhaps he had come into the *Blackbirds* on chance and her father had offered to show him the castle, and that what they were both discussing was really something to do with her mother's birthday and nothing at all suspicious? But Lucy could not convince herself that this was so. The man with her father, who had left him so rudely when Humf had run up to them, had been showing something as furtively as he had just been spying round this house. Had Humf, in his anger and disappointment, come back here, and had this man, recognising him, hidden him away somewhere to ask him questions about their father?

Then Lucy realised she was being ridiculous and dramatic. Humf had run off in a temper and was probably at the camp by now and she could, after all, have been mistaken by the man at the window. He might even be a man who lived in a nearby cottage and helped Mr. Strang with the turkeys!

So she ran across the yard shouting, "Don't hide from me, Humf! It's me, Lucy. The others are sorry and want you back at the camp."

There was no reply, but as she hurried round the corner of the house she noticed in the dust the track left by the tyres of a bicycle and then she saw, half in and half out of her kennel, the body of the bitch Jess. She was lying on her side and as Lucy, horror-struck, called her by name she realised that she was quite still and that a few flies were buzzing round her head.

She went down on her knees and gently touched the silky head. There was no sign of a wound although Jess lay as if she had been struck down with a sudden blow. Lucy knew now who was cowardly enough to kill a chained dog so close to the time when her puppies were to be born.

Then she heard a car and as she got up Mr. Strang, with his wife beside him, stopped his old car and got out.

Lucy ran to him and his comforting arm held her as she tried to tell her story.

"That awful man," she sobbed. "He must have murdered Jess. I've just found her like this. We've lost Humf, and I came to the house and the kitchen door was open so I went in and called for him and then I saw that wicked man glaring at me——"

"Steady, Lucinda," Mr. Strang said. "You're safe now and we'll soon find your brother. Take her in, Susan, and let me look at Jess first."

"But she's dead," Lucy sobbed. "He's murdered her and her puppies and all for nothing because I'm sure she never did anybody any harm . . . I've got the key. I remembered to lock the door. You're not angry with me, are you?"

"No, Lucinda," Susan Strang said quietly. "Nobody is angry, and we think you've been brave. Try not to cry and tell me quietly and sensibly exactly what has happened. There's nothing now to fear if you're sure nobody is in the house."

Lucy gulped, felt in vain for a handkerchief, wiped her eyes with one grubby hand and found to her surprise that the other was held firmly by Mrs. Strang.

"He came on a bike," she said quietly. "He must have done. You can see the marks of the tyres in the dust. I only remembered after, but Jess didn't bark when I came."

"Give me the key," Mrs. Strang said. "We'll talk about this indoors and then we'll fetch the others . . . What about Jess, George?"

The farmer got up and smiled at Lucy.

"She's not dead. I reckon she's been drugged. Open the door and I'll telephone Harry Gibbs, the vet . . . No, wait. I'll go round the house first just to make sure . . . At the top of the lane you will remember, Susan, we passed a disreputable young man on a bicycle. Perhaps we will also telephone the police."

By the time the Strangs had made sure that nobody was hiding in the house and that nothing had been disturbed, they realised that Jess was recovering. Nevertheless, Mr. Strang telephoned for the vet who promised to come at once.

"Now, Lucinda," the farmer said as he replaced the receiver. "I do not like the idea of this strange young man. We have been warned about strangers poking round, but I think you should go back to your camp and see if your brother has returned. If he has not, go out with John and Peggy and look for him. Mrs. Strang will go with you now to the camp and bring a message back to me."

"But the adders?" Lucy faltered. "Humf might have got bitten and he wouldn't do all the things to himself that John explained. And do you think we ought to telephone Conways and let my parents know that Humf has disappeared?"

Mrs. Strang smiled at her reassuringly and put her hand through her arm. As they walked together down the field she said:

"Don't worry so much, my dear. It's easy to get the paths mixed up in your mind in the forest. We shall find your brother and there are some people round here who talk too much about adders. John Hogben is a sensible lad and can find his way about, and I promise we'll telephone the foresters and get some help if we haven't found the lad soon . . . Why you four should like sleeping and eating out of doors down here is more than I can guess. My bed is good enough for me . . . I can smell wood smoke now, so run ahead and see if the boy is there."

Mrs. Strang was so quiet and sensible that she made Lucy feel better. This was as well because Humf had not come back and John and Peggy seemed rather peeved at being left alone for so long to do the chores.

"It's no use saying that you think Humf is a nuisance even if you think so," Lucy said sharply. "It was your fault he ran off, and now the Strangs' dog Jess has been poisoned and I saw a strange man poking round Pollards . . . Here's Mrs. Strang now and she'll tell you that what I say is true. I'm not interested in camping until we find Humf . . . The dog isn't dead anyway."

John, who had been chopping up some of the larger pieces of dead wood put down the chopper.

"Sorry, Lucy. Maybe I shouted at Humf. We'll stop everything and find him. He can't have gone far and it won't be dark for two or three hours yet. What about you, Mrs. Strang? Will you come with us or ask your husband to telephone for more help. My father would come, I'm sure, and the foresters are used to people losing themselves. Sorry about Jess. That's bad. She would have helped . . . Damp down the fire, Peg. We'll have our bangers when we've found Humf. We'll give him a real feast."

Mrs. Strang made no answer for a long minute.

Lucy watched her as she looked at the lowering sky above the tree tops and wondered what she was thinking about. She struggled to remember the word that described her. Suddenly it came—the word was "serene." Then she felt Peggy's hand touch hers and heard her whisper, "Sorry, Lucy. We were foul to Humf. I'm sure we'll soon find him. We'll each take a different path and call and whistle and keep in touch with each other. John knows the forest and Humf can't have gone far."

Lucy squeezed her fingers as Mrs. Strang remarked, "This is a very big forest for a small boy who hasn't been here before. I shall tell my husband that you are searching now but ask him to call up the foresters and possibly the police. And I think, Lucinda, that your parents should be told. I feel sure that you have nothing to be really anxious about but keep your heads . . . Cover that fire with stones and as there will probably be a thunderstorm it would be better if you all came back to the house as soon as you find the boy . . . Good luck."

They watched her walk back up the meadow, and as the sky was suddenly lit up by a great flash of lightning John said briskly, "Come on. We'll find him. Wish we'd got Mark though. We could do with one more, specially as you don't know the forest, Lucy . . . You're not sulking, are you? I've said we're sorry. I thought young Humf was enjoying himself."

"She's not sulking," Peggy said. "Humf is her brother and she's sort of responsible for him. You're not really worried about him are you, John?"

"Not really. I don't know him well enough. I'm not sure about the adders in this hot thundery weather. Wish it would rain. What d'you think he'd do, Lucy? He's a sensible kid and surely if he's lost he'll shout?"

"That will be fine if there's anybody to hear him,"

Lucy said. "Tell us what to do, John, and we'll start shouting. You're not the only one who wishes Mark was here . . . Oh dear! We keep saying we're sorry to each other. I know you understand now how I feel about Humf. He's sensible enough and I don't think he'd rush about in a panic. Tell us what to do, John."

He led them first up the narrow path from what Lucy called the "Adder Gate." It was easy to see where the boy had crawled under some of the conifers and filled his sack with twigs and brown, crisp fir cones. Obviously he went no further than he need to do his chore and he had left some signs on the grassy track where he had dragged his load. John explained that this path was really a short cut to Pollards from one of the big rides and was rarely used. There were no defined tracks between the rows of trees and there would be no particular reason for Humf to leave the path.

They stopped several times and called his name but there was no response. The wood was very quiet, and the heavy air of the impending storm seemed to stifle their voices, and eventually they reached the first big ride where Humf had recovered most of his usual good humour. They rested here too, and John explained how the rides divided the forest into big squares so that fire fighting equipment and tractors, hauling mowers to keep the grass short, could travel quickly from one danger spot to another. At the junction of most of the big rides were iron water tanks at one of which, he suggested, Humf might be resting.

Lucy believed that having decided to run off, Humf would go as far and as fast as he could, always hoping that he would meet somebody and ask the way out of the forest. She did not believe now that the red-headed man she had seen at Pollards had anything to do with Humf's disappearance, but she did not want to tell the others more about the stranger nor that she had seen him before.

On the side of one of the big water tanks John, with a piece of chalk scratched a rough plan of the rides in the forest and it was Peggy's idea that they should add a message—HUMF, WE ARE SEARCHING FOR YOU. PLEASE GO BACK TO POLLARDS DOWN THE HILL FIRST TRACK ON RIGHT. ANSWER IF YOU HEAR US CALLING.

"Might as well write him a letter," Lucy observed. "We'd all better take a lump of chalk and write a message on every tank. But we can't keep saying 'First turning on right' can we?"

By now both the Hogbens were worried. John was nervous about the adders and wouldn't admit it, and Peggy felt guilty about the way in which they had neglected Humf and was frightened for Lucy's sake. After the first message had been written, John showed them how one of them was to walk to the top of the ride and the other to the bottom, calling for Humf at intervals. Neither was to take any of the side tracks and if they met anybody they must describe Humf and ask if he had been seen. He showed them on his rough map how downhill the grassy rides led eventually to the main road, and up, to the north, to another ride which was the boundary of the forest. He was going to take the continuation of the Pollards path until he came to the next north-south ride and mark another tank before exploring the full length of that one.

"It's almost at the top of that ride that there are four big trees which give the name to Deadman's Wood," John explained. "They were there long before the rest of the forest was planted, and just because they are rather a landmark Humf may have made for them. They stand high and I reckon that's the sort of place I'd look for if I was lost and he was fascinated by the story of the smugglers, wasn't he?"

The girls nodded.

"We've all got watches," John went on. "Whoever finds Humf or gets any clue must keep on shouting for the others. If Humf is hurt we'll have to use our wits, but this corner here with the first message must be our meeting place. If we're in real trouble and have to get him back to Pollards, one of us will have to run back first for help. And of course we can all add another message to the tank. Jim, the forester, has a horse so he's the chap we want to meet although, as Peggy remembers, his house is miles away near the main entrance . . . So let's go now and be back here within three-quarters of an hour."

Lucy set off downhill feeling thoroughly disheartened and unhappy. She hated the forest, wished they had gone camping at the sea and she still missed Mark. And she was really frightened because Humf might by now be in real trouble.

They had arranged to call his name every fifty paces. Her own voice sounded feeble and after about three hundred yards she couldn't even hear Peggy. After each call she strained her ears and she was the first to hear a dog bark, although she could not be sure in which direction. She heard John's next call, faint and far away to her left and decided sensibly to run back to the tank where they had left the first message and add a few more words about the dog's bark for the others. She was breathless when she got there after running uphill, and was glad to see Peggy hurrying down towards her. When she saw Lucy she rushed down to her excitedly. She had not heard the bark nor met anyone, but announced that she had reached the edge of the forest and seen open country ahead.

"Just like the downs at Conways, Lucy. I'm sure Humf wouldn't go out that way, although I could see one farm a long way off. There's no road he could take except another path at the very edge of the forest as John told us. I heard him calling once or twice but can't hear him now. Shall we chalk another message and go to meet him? We must tell him you heard a dog. Do you know what sort of dog? . . . Sorry, that was a silly suggestion. What shall we do?"

"That dog has reminded me of the police dog Humf told me about yesterday. The dog called Dandy," Lucy explained. "You know that girl Betsy Maycock at school, Peg? I b'lieve it's her dad who looks after that dog and that's what we want now. It's getting darker and I'm sure we must telephone somewhere for help. I must tell my parents, Peg, and if you like I'll run back to Pollards and tell them and you wait for John . . . Let's shout for him together now. For John I mean."

This time they were successful and not only heard his answering shout but a few seconds later heard it repeated and then they saw him running towards them. They ran to meet him, and while he was struggling to find enough breath to speak, Lucy told him about the dog she was sure she had heard barking far away to the south.

He nodded and then gasped out his news.

"I've found where Humf has been, I reckon . . . Some fool of a picknicker must have left a broken bottle under the four trees of Deadman's Wood. There was blood on some of the grass and the grass was trampled . . . I shouted but there was no reply. I searched all round wondering if he'd crawled away but I couldn't see any more blood . . ."

"He was wearing sandals," Lucy whispered. "He never wears socks. Where could he go if he cut his foot badly? How far have you searched, John? We don't even know if the blood is his. We don't know whether he's been found, but I'll tell you what I'm going to do. I'm going to run back to Pollards and fetch Mr. Strang and we'll telephone for somebody who will really do something."

". . . That's not fair," Peggy broke in indignantly. "Humf needn't have run off like that in a temper, and John *has* done something. All the same it is a good idea for one of us to tell the Strangs what John has found . . . Are you sure you heard the dog in the south, Lucy?"

"No, I'm not. I'm not sure of anything except that something serious must have happened to Humf. I know I heard a dog bark, but we can't even hear our own shouts properly in these trees can we? No, you two go back to the Deadman's trees and search every inch and I'll run back to Pollards. I know the way and can't get lost and if you find Humf you'll know I'll have got there first. If they've any news we'll come at once and find you. O.K.?"

John was so surprised at 'Little Lucy' taking control like this that he could only nod and give her a smile of encouragement as she turned and ran back to the ride where they had marked the first tank. She turned once to wave but wasted no time by chalking another message. She was more confident now about her brother, feeling sure that somebody had found him and was helping him. She knew that no cars were allowed in the forest, but a forester on a horse would make a wonderful rescuer, but it *was* strange that none of them had found it easy to hear each other in the hot, sultry air of the forest. She even began to wonder whether she really had heard that dog or only imagined it. And then, when she had nearly reached the 'adder gate' she met Mr. Strang and when she saw his slow smile of welcome she knew that the news was good.

Suddenly his arms were round her, and while she tried to find the breath to speak she heard him say, "Now, now, my dear. Your brother is safe. He cut his foot and a police dog on training exercise in the forest found him. The dog's handler carried him back to the car, and a radio message was telephoned through to us to say he was being taken to hospital, then to see his parents. And if all is as well as they think, he insists on being brought back here tonight. I've got a high opinion of these police chaps and they seem to think very well of your brother. They say he won't be parted from the dog who found him . . . Now, Lucinda. You mustn't spoil good news by crying down my shirt."

"I'm not really crying. I'm happy. You're so kind and clever at doing things at once. We only met you and Mrs. Strang a few hours ago and it's as if we've always known you . . . It's wonderful."

"Yes, Lucinda," Mr. Strang said quietly as he disengaged himself and wiped her face with his own handkerchief. "What you say is true. To feel like this is wonderful. Some people call it friendship. Others, like my wife and myself who are much more old-fashioned, call it love. When you are older you will know what I mean . . . Now where are the Hogbens?"

She smiled up at him, but when she had told him their adventures, she realised that she hadn't asked about Jess, nor if there was any news of the red-haired man.

"Jess will be all right, the vet thinks. She's been poisoned with something probably given her on a bit of meat. Must have been that man you saw and we met in the lane. I've told the police about him and they were interested . . . Now you go back to Mrs. Strang and tell her I've gone on to find John and Peggy. The storm is moving away and with luck you'll have your camp tonight . . . Now, cheer up, love. We're all friends here, aren't we? Remember what I said."

She walked slowly back through the adder gate and past the deserted camp.

'We're all friends here,' he had said, but she still did not want the Hogbens to ask too many questions about the man who had been talking secretly to her father and now, it seemed, had deliberately drugged a dog.

Mrs. Strang was knitting under the roses which covered the porch of Pollards and smiled as Lucy ran up to her.

"I can see you've met my husband and had the good news of that brother of yours. He'll be here soon so just sit down quietly and tell me all about yourself, and how you all got into this muddle on the first day of your holidays . . . And wait awhile until you've cooled down before you fetch yourself some of the lemonade I made for you this morning. Where are the others?"

Lucy fetched a cushion and sat at her new friend's feet and told her how frightened they had been in the forest and of how John had found the blood-stained broken glass.

"You've made me feel so much better," she finished. "Thank you for being so kind, and I'm afraid we're rather a nuisance to you . . . And I haven't asked you about Jess yet. Mr. Strang said she'd been poisoned."

"Yes, she has, and our friend the vet has taken her home with him, but he thinks she'll do. Do you think your mother would let you have one of her pups, if they're born safe and sound? Just to remind you of us?"

"I don't think Mum would think it a good idea at the *Blackbirds*, thank you all the same. There isn't really much room and there are such a lot of stairs . . . And we've got a cat called Pickwick . . . Look, Mrs. Strang. Here are the others coming up the hill and I can hear a police car or an ambulance tooting. I bet that's Humf."

Sure enough, as John and Peggy, both looking exceedingly hot and tired followed Mr. Strang through the gate up to the house, a smart blue and white panda car drew up in the yard with the blue lamp flashing on the roof. Humf, they observed, was sitting in the front seat with the driver looking pleased with himself. What was more, he was smug and obviously intended to make the most of such a dramatic situation.

When the car stopped, the constable in the back seat got out, opened the door for Humf and helped him to the ground. He looked cleaner than usual and was wearing a shirt which Lucy knew he had left at home, a sandal on the uninjured foot and an old soft rubber shoe on the other.

The policeman saluted Mrs. Strang.

"Delivering Mr. Humphrey Brown as directed, Madam. Victim has been discharged from hospital, inspected by parents and warned against overstrain and overwork."

The rather long silence that followed as Humf beamed at them all was broken by John who was not feeling or looking his best.

"And where are his crutches, constable?" he asked. "Poor little chap. And wasn't there an ambulance to spare?"

"Ha! Ha!" Humf remarked cautiously. "Ha, jolly ha! You think you're funny John, but it's not your fault I haven't been bitten by a nadder. This forest is full of nadders. You ask this super police driver who let me do the siren thing just to let you know I was coming. He says the whole forest is crawling with nadders and it ought to be closed up and made a nadder reserve . . . That's what you said, wasn't it, Robert?" he added to their surprise. And then, even more unexpectedly, "His name is Robert—not Bob."

Driver Pinder looked a little embarrassed.

"Not exactly, son . . . I'm to tell you, Mr. Strang, that he cut his foot on broken glass up in Deadman's Wood. We can't seem to teach picnickers to take their bottles and rubbish home with them. He hasn't told us how long he was there, but he was found by one of our dogs who were training in the forest. His handler got the message through soon as he'd carried the lad back to his van. They've put a couple of stitches in the cut at the hospital and given him an injection. He's O.K. but he wouldn't go into Casualty without the dog Dandy who found him. He's seen his parents and because he wanted to get back here they agreed and send their thanks. So here he is but before we leave, we'd like a private word with you and Mrs. Strang. There's the matter of the chap you described, sir, and the poisoned bitch . . ."

Mr. Strang nodded and led the second constable indoors while Driver Robert Pinder got back into the car and called Police Headquarters on his radio telephone to report his position. Then he nodded to the four children and stayed in the car which was a good hint that light conversation was over for the present.

"I could do with a drink, but I reckon we'd better not go into the house yet," John said. "Let's go over and sit on the wall and Humf can tell us all about the nadders that didn't bite him."

Peggy glanced at Humf and saw the quick look he gave his sister.

"O.K., John," she said. "Humf has had enough . . . Thanks for all the wood you collected, Humf. We'll soon get the fire going again and there are bangers for for supper. Let's forget the nadders."

"Fair enough," John agreed and lifted Humf on to the garden wall. "We can't have a proper camp without a wood and water carrier and you've done your share, big boy. Now tell us about the dog and how many miles you ran through the forest. About a nundred I s'pose?"

So peace was signed and Lucy, in particular, encouraged her brother to talk about Dandy. She didn't want the others to refer to the red-headed man. In fact, she didn't want Humf to know about him in case he asked, straight out, whether this was the same man they had seen with their father.

It so happened that Humf was now so glad to be back and pleased that John was no longer angry with him, that he would have talked only about Dandy and his handler Sergeant Maycock for an hour. He was interrupted however after ten minutes when Mr. Strang came to the door of the house and called to Lucy.

"Just Lucinda, please. Constable Harris thinks you can help him."

The others glanced at her curiously as she jumped off the wall and ran to Mr. Strang waiting for her in the porch.

"Nothing to worry about, my dear," he said. "The police are interested in the young man who we are sure poisoned Jess and watched you through the window. You arc the only one of us who saw him clearly and they want a description."

There was nothing frightening about the scene in the sitting-room. Mrs. Strang smiled at her reassuringly over her knitting, the policeman with his cap and an open notebook on the table beside him had obviously been enjoying a glass of lemonade, and his smile was just as friendly when he spoke to her.

"We want you to help us, please Lucy. You know that Mr. Strang's bitch must have been poisoned by the man you saw, and who Mr. and Mrs. Strang met on a bicycle in the lane. They couldn't see him clearly, but perhaps you can remember him better because you were a bit scared. Sometimes it's easier to remember people and things when you're surprised and frightened. I know that happens to me sometimes . . . Please try to tell me what he looked like. Was his hair long or short? What was he wearing? That's the sort of thing we want to know."

If he was surprised at the skill of Lucy's description, he didn't at first show it. Having been asked straightforward questions and wanting this interview over as soon as possible, Lucy never realised that her first impressions of the man, when she had seen him at the castle, were most vivid.

So she described him well. The longish, unkempt, reddish hair with side-whiskers and the dark specs. "He took those off, but I don't know the colour of his eyes. And I couldn't guess his age but he wasn't old. Sort of thirty, I suppose. And he was wearing a coloured shirt with a pattern on it—and blue jeans . . . That's all I can remember."

The constable looked at her curiously.

"That's clever of you, Lucy. Thank you for remembering so well. Mr. Strang showed me the kitchen. Can you remember where you were standing when you heard him outside and turned round and saw him staring at you through the window?"

"Over by the stairs, I think. I believe I'd called out for Humf or Mrs. Strang. Why is that important?"

She noticed the grown-ups glance at each other and then the constable said, "Would you mind coming into the kitchen with me, Lucy. I'll stand outside the window and you stay by the stairs where you were when you saw him."

Lucy was puzzled but did as she was asked and the others came with her. The policemen went outside, she stopped at the bottom of the stairs and called her brother's name, and when she heard the scrape of a footstep outside she turned and saw the constable smiling, not scowling like the other man, at her through the kitchen window. She saw his face quite clearly and when he came back she told him so.

"Yes. Just like you were standing only he had dark specs on."

"As tall as I was, Lucy?"

"About the same, I think. And then he must have gone off on a bike which he'd left somewhere. Have I told you all you want to know and may I go with the others now?"

"Yes, Lucy. Almost everything. You've been a great help, and I must tell you that we think this man is working with a woman thief along the south coast. She is an artist and stops at places like this to ask if she can paint the house, and this would be an excuse for getting in and to see if there is anything worth stealing. We're not sure yet what this young man is actually doing and how he is working with her, but from what you've told us it seems as if he was spying round to see if the house was empty and you surprised him. But one thing still puzzles me, Lucy. You were sure he was wearing blue jeans, but how can you be certain if you only saw his head through the window? You didn't see him ride off on his bike, did you? You said that it was when he saw *you* that he made off. Try to help us, Lucy. We want to talk to this man. If you're sure he was wearing blue jeans, where have you seen him before?"

Lucy was horrified into silence. What could she say? What had her father been doing with a man wanted by the police?

5

Thursday: "That's what Dandy told us !"

BREAKFAST at the *Blackbirds* the following morning was certainly quieter than when Lucy and Humf were there, fighting their daily battle against time. This battle was not merely to eat enough before the eventual last moment before leaving for school. Lucy had further to go and left first, but Humf enjoyed a leisurely meal with some conversation. He knew that his mother wished him to make a good start of the day with a hearty meal but was always too busy to listen to him. Lucy, he believed, was selfishly concerned with her own affairs, such as what she must remember to take to school or remember to bring back, or could she bring a friend into the café for an ice if she paid for it.

Through all this turmoil, their father also talked or read extracts from the paper. Occasionally the post arrived before the children left, and although the letters received by Mervyn Brown seemed to depress him as much as the news, something urged him to comment on his mail as well.

But on this particular morning when the children were away, neither of their parents had been able to sleep later than usual, and although Mr. Brown offered to bring his wife breakfast in bed she was more worried about what would happen to his own. Besides, she wanted to talk to him about the children, and was still worried about Humf and all the fuss last evening about his cut foot. She knew that she would not be able to relax in bed or talk to Mervyn while she could hear him grumbling in their little kitchen and pretending that he didn't know where anything was kept. So she thanked him and noticed his relief, and cooked bacon and eggs for them both without the usual battle against time.

Elsie arrived about nine to clean the café while Mrs. Brown started her baking of scones and cakes for which she was becoming well known in the town. Today, there was over an hour before she need start work.

Mervyn, after a hurried glance at the newspaper, flung it on the floor—some men would have folded it and put it on the table, others would have just dropped it, Mervyn rejected it dramatically. Then he smiled at his wife.

"Mary, my dear! How agreeable to have an hour like this. You are a wonderful wife and I am an impossible husband. You have forgiven me so many times for reading at meals that I dare not ask you to do so again. I have been wondering what would please you best as a birthday celebration on Saturday. I have some ideas, but I suppose we cannot afford to close the café or ask Elsie to take sole charge?"

"Oh, Mervyn, of course we can't. You know that we aren't yet really paying our way, but we are doing better and there are lots of visitors in the town. Please don't worry about my birthday and you're not to give me anything special. Perhaps we could do something with the children in the evening? . . . And that reminds me. Do you think it's too early to go out and telephone those nice Strangs and see if Humf is all right?"

"But of course he is, Mary. You must not fuss over the boy. He's been to hospital, the cut was stitched and they gave him an anti-tetanus injection. Nobody could do more. Humphrey is no longer a baby, and although it sounds absurd to say that he can stand on his own feet when it appears that he can't without wounding himself, he must learn not to rely on his sister and her older friends. He's an intelligent boy, Mary, and we must not spoil him."

"I suppose not, but he *is* rather young for the Hogbens and Mark . . . I didn't ask you last night when he insisted on going back to their camp, but I did wonder why the others allowed him to go off by himself. And did you hear him say that the forest was full of adders and that they nail them up on gate posts?"

"Of course I did, and it's true that foresters do display dead adders as a warning to walkers. Surely you're not suggesting that he was bitten by an adder? Humphrey must learn by experience, my dear. I do my best to instruct him in ways in which only a father can . . ."

"Of course you do, Mervyn. I'm not really anxious about the children but I miss them. Do you realise how much we owe to many new friends like the vicar and his wife and of course the Hogbens for their kindness to Lucy and Humf."

"Yes, yes, Mary. My appreciation of their courtesy has inspired my brilliant idea for your birthday celebration. Apart from my own, and our children's small tributes, I thought that we, as a family, might organise a barbecue party and invite all the children's friends, although I am not sure whether Mark Simson will have left with his parents by that time . . . No, my dear. Please let me finish. I have heard of a small cove below the cliffs near Greenhaven—I believe it was once used by smugglers—and this seems an ideal spot after sundown. Quite an adventure, in fact. We should have to make arrangements for the actual grill but I've no doubt I could borrow one. We should have a fire of driftwood, Mary, and if the tide is right and the sea not too rough we might swim . . . Yes, the more I consider this the more certain I am that this would not only be an ideal celebration of your birthday but a way of showing our thanks to the Hogbens and others who have befriended our children. We shall have to discuss the matter of transport and of course the provisions——"

"Mervyn dear, *please* forget this idea. It would be lovely for me just to have the evening with the three of you. Just a walk on the downs or even a bus to Brighton, but *please* not anything which means the preparation of more food. A barbecue isn't as easy as it sounds and it would mean quite a lot of food, and I think it's a long way down to Smugglers Cove carrying everything . . . And anyway the children are already camping and I really do have enough cooking to do all day . . . I know you are going to say that you and the children will do everything while I sit down quietly and watch you . . . But I'm an interfering woman really, and——"

At this moment the doorbell rang. Not once, but three peals which suggested urgency.

"No, Mervyn. I'll go. It might be Win Robson with a telephone message from Pollards. Perhaps Humf is really ill," and she was halfway down the stairs before her husband was out of his chair.

He went to the landing and to his amazement heard Lucinda's voice: "I'm so pleased to see you, Mum. No. Nothing awful has happened. Yes, Humf is O.K. I'm all right really but Mrs. Strang gave me some breakfast and told me where to get the first bus to Malling. Is Dad upstairs?"

"But darling Lucy, why have you come home? You've been crying. What's happened? You know you can tell me everything."

"It's terribly difficult to explain, Mum, but you must trust me. I haven't really any secrets from you, but this is something I must tell Dad first. *I just have to do this* . . . No, I haven't really run away. Mrs. Strang knows I've come back to see Dad, and I promise that Humf is just as bouncy as usual if not more so, and everybody is very kind."

Mervyn from the top of the stairs broke a long silence.

"Come up, Lucinda. Come and tell us everything."

He went back into the sitting room and was shocked at the sight of her pale and tear-stained face. Compassion and love for his only daughter brought a lump to his throat, and as he stepped forward Lucy flung her arms round him.

He held her close and looked over her head at his wife.

"Leave the breakfast things," she said quietly. "I'll be in the café, but call me at once if you want me . . . Lucy dear. Before you speak to your father you *must* answer one question. Do the others know where you are?"

Lucy gulped and lifted her face from her father's chest.

"Yes, Mum. I woke Peggy early in the tent because I couldn't sleep. I told her that I must come home at once and see dad, and she said, 'Well, if you must you must, and if you can't tell me what's wrong I s'pose I can wait. I'll tell the boys when they wake.' And she said to run up and tell Mrs. Strang who would be up by now. And she was, and she didn't ask unkind questions and made me eat an egg and said she'd tell Mr. Strang when he came back from his turkeys . . . It's just that I must talk to Dad first, Mum. Please try to understand."

Mrs. Brown nodded—not quite so sympathetically as usual—and closed the door quietly behind her.

In spite of his many short-comings, Mervyn Brown

could sometimes forget himself and his wild plans and hopes. But he rarely forgot his family, and in this sudden crisis he was at his best.

He felt in his pocket for a handkerchief which, as usual, was somewhere else.

"Go and wash your face and hands and do something to your hair, Lucy, and you'll feel better. If you have done anything wrong, or of which you are ashamed, we shall stand by you. If you want to share somebody else's secret we will try to keep it, and if you want help for yourself, or for your friends or for somebody we don't know we'll try to help. I know you will tell us the truth but there are one or two special things for you to remember. First, I have no serious secrets from your mother and secondly I expect you to tell me everything that is worrying you. *Everything*. Do you promise?"

For the first time for hours she smiled and nodded. When she came back five minutes later she was still pale but more composed. Meanwhile Mervyn had washed up the breakfast things.

"Now, Lucy," he smiled. "Tell me all and remember that your mother is waiting to hear what you cannot tell us together. You're not afraid now, are you? Sit down. I've made some more coffee so we'll have some together.

Lucy sat down, and as she lifted her cup and looked at her father she smiled because she knew that he couldn't possibly do anything as wrong as the awful suspicions which had been worrying her ever since she had seen him with the stranger in the castle grounds. Impetuously she ran round the table and kissed his cheek which still smelled of the shaving lotion she remembered since she was a baby.

"You must forgive me, Dad, for the awful things I have been thinking. I had to speak to you first because you said that your business with that red-headed man had something to do with Mum's birthday and that we weren't to say anything more about it. You were cross too and Humf and I saw him take something out of his pocket sort of secretly and show you . . . And yesterday I saw that same man spying round Pollards Farm where we're camping. And he saw me and ran off and the awful thing, Dad, is that the police want to see him because they think he's got something to do with stealing precious things from lonely houses . . . And the policeman who brought Humf back last night asked me about the man. And I was a coward and I've done very, very wrong. When he asked me if I'd seen the man before, because he seemed to have recognised me, I got mixed up and said 'No, I hadn't.' "

"I see," her father said slowly. "You denied recognising him because you thought I might have something to do with a man wanted by the police?"

She nodded miserably. "I s'pose that was it. He was a horrible man. He looked as if he hated us and I've been so miserable about the lie I told that I had to see you first. You see, somebody must tell the police that you've seen him . . . And if he's stealing from houses, you wouldn't know unless I told you what they think, would you?"

"No, Lucy. I wouldn't know so soon anyway. You are a brave and honest girl and before we tell your mother everything together, I must tell you that I bought from that man a very beautiful little box which he sold to me for an absurd price and which I intended to give your mother for her birthday on Saturday. Now it seems I might be a receiver of stolen goods. Of course we must tell the police at once and return the box to them, but before we do I would like to show your mother the present I cannot now give her and together we must tell her the whole story. I will fetch her and if you will look in the right-hand drawer of my chest in our bedroom, you will find, hidden under my ties a small parcel in tissue paper secured with two elastic bands. Bring it down, my dear. It is a snuff-box of the Regency period—a genuine and most beautiful treasure."

Lucy found the little parcel in the drawer where she knew her father kept the very few articles which he treasured most. It was not heavy and through the wrapping she could feel that it was round. She believed that it was going to lead to trouble and perhaps spoil their little holiday and her mother's birthday. She didn't dare to think how much her father had paid for something stolen, nor even to suggest that however beautiful it might be, there were so many other gifts which would be more acceptable to her hard-working mother. Lucy didn't know anything about Regency snuff-boxes but was sure that she wouldn't know what to do with it. Then she heard her name called and ran down to her parents and passed the package to her father.

"I haven't looked at it, Dad . . . Has he told you everything, Mum? You do understand, don't you? It was awful for me not to tell you both together, but I knew there was a secret about your birthday."

"Yes, Lucy, I understand. Before we tell the police and show them the snuff-box, we must be sure who else knows about this."

"Humf saw the man with me at the castle, but not yesterday. I haven't told the Hogbens anything—or Mark, 'cos I haven't seen him, but I think I would have done if he'd been with us. I didn't tell Mr. and Mrs. Strang or the policeman that I'd seen that man before. I told them that he was wearing blue jeans which I couldn't have seen through the kitchen window. I must have just remembered that's how he was dressed when he was with Dad . . ."

"What about Elsie?" Mrs. Brown asked. "I told her that the police have asked us all to look out for a grey-haired woman artist. I suppose this man is working for her? Mervyn, you are so very sweet to think of giving me such a present, but it must go to the police at once, and as we're not on the telephone yet you had better take it round with Lucy."

"But don't you want to *see* the box?" Mervyn gasped. "This assumption that I am in possession of stolen goods may be entirely incorrect. I admit that Lucy's sight of the young man yesterday at Pollards is a coincidence, but I really must explain to you both that there was nothing suspicious about the man when he came into the café on the morning you went to Brighton. I can't agree with Lucinda's suggestion that he was horrible. He came in for a coffee, I attended to his needs, and in the course of an agreeable conversation he admitted that he was a stranger to Malling and was interested in old and historic places and works of art. Naturally I asked him if he would like to see the castle and he was pleased to accept my offer. On the way we stopped to glance in the window of Binfield's antique shop and found we had another interest in common. I happened to mention that I was looking for something rare and beautiful and he admitted that he was temporarily in need of cash, and had something in his pocket which he was thinking of offering to an expert. Naturally I asked if I might see it and now, my dear, I show it you just in case the man was untruthful and that this lovely snuff-box did not belong to his great-grandfather and was bequeathed to him . . . Open it now, Mary. This may have been used by a courtier of the Prince Regent at the Royal Pavilion at Brighton only a few miles away, or in the Assembly

Rooms at Tunbridge Wells or even by Beau Nash himself at Bath . . . Open it, my dear."

Mary Brown kissed him.

"You are a kind but hopeless husband, Mervyn. You cannot possibly afford a Regency snuff-box, and even if you could I don't take snuff and have not enough valuable jewellery to keep in it! Let us look at it together and then you and Lucy must take it back to the police station. Tell them that we were warned yesterday by a panda crew about a woman artist who may be a thief. Mrs. Hogben was here at the time and I think the constable's name was Harris. He told us to get in touch with the police station if we had anything to report. Now let's see the treasure and say goodbye to it. I'm sure the police will want to question that young man as soon as possible, but it's odd that they did not mention him yesterday."

They were all silent as she took off the elastic bands and removed the tissue paper which fluttered to the floor. At first sight the box was not exciting. It was circular and about three inches across and made of dark brown tortoiseshell. Round the rim of the lid was a raised design of dull gold-like metal in the shape of a plaited cord, but within this circlet was an exquisite miniature painting of a young woman with blonde hair in ringlets and very blue eyes. She was not particularly beautiful but the artist had caught the girl's pleasant smile.

"Of course I cannot be sure yet, my dear, but I have been wondering whether the portrait which is undoubtedly of the Regency period might not be of Princess Charlotte herself. I must have this examined. The Curator of the Brighton Museum would know——"

"But, dearest Mervyn, this may not be ours . . ."

Lucy said nothing. Snuff-boxes meant nothing to

her and she had never seen one before, but what her mother was now holding might well be valuable. What could have made her father believe that the red-headed man would sell such a lovely thing to a stranger? Of course he was as likely to be fooled by anybody who had something to sell which appealed to him, and she knew that even this purchase had been inspired because he wanted to plan a lovely birthday surprise.

Tears stung her eyes as she saw that her mother's were as wet, and she turned to run from the room. What her parents were saying to each other was no business of hers, but she had done what she had to do and as she sat on her bed waiting to be called she wondered just how much Humf had suspected—or cared—what it was that the stranger had sold to their father. Of course everything would be all right once the horrid little thing had been given back to the police, but she still hoped that she wouldn't have to tell either Mark or the Hogbens about what had happened.

Then she heard her father calling her, and as soon as she saw him taking his old panama hat from the peg on the landing she knew he was in a jaunty mood, and was now prepared not only to overlook his own mistakes but to take control of the whole affair.

"There is nothing for you to be upset about now my dear," he said. "Nothing at all. It seems that the snuff-box might have been stolen, and your mother thinks it would be a good idea if you came along to the police station with me. They will obviously appreciate the help I can give them. If indeed this trinket has been stolen, then no doubt, although you did not see the man as clearly as I did, your description of him will be helpful. There's nothing for you to worry about, Lucinda."

"Oh, Dad. Please don't talk in that sort of cheerful

way. Of course I'm coming with you. Can't you see that I told the policeman at Pollards last night that I hadn't seen that awful man before. At least even if I didn't actually tell such a lie, I didn't tell him the truth when he asked where I'd seen him before. I explained all that just now. You know that I came away from Pollards early so that I could talk to you first . . . I must see that nice constable with you and we can explain together why I thought the thief was wearing blue jeans. Let's go at once. I'm not afraid if you're there, but I do want to get it over and go back to the others, please. They don't know why I've come. I just told Mrs. Strang and Peggy that I had to see you urgently but would be coming back . . . Where's Mum?"

"In the kitchen with Elsie. She thinks it would be wiser if Elsie did not know why you had come home early."

Malling had a smart new police station which was light and bright and cheerful inside. A young constable behind a counter greeted them with a polite "Good morning, sir. What can we do for you?" and a winning smile for Lucy.

"I am confident, Constable, that there is a great deal I can do for you. I ask for an immediate interview with your Station Officer on a matter of extreme importance. My name is Mervyn Brown of the *Four & Twenty Blackbirds* in Pottery Lane, and I have reason to believe that, quite innocently, I have in my possession a valuable trinket that may have been stolen. This is my daughter Lucinda, who also has some information which may assist your enquiries."

This was certainly one of Mervyn's best speeches, and Lucy knew that he was now enjoying himself.

"Quite so, Mr. Brown. Have you been in touch with your area constable or any of our panda cars?"

"I am not yet connected to the telephone service, officer, but my wife has told me that she was visited yesterday by a Constable Harris. I thought it best to take complete control of this situation myself. I have the article in my pocket and have called here at some personal inconvenience to place myself at the disposal of the police."

"Quite so, Mr. Brown. If you will wait a moment I will see if our station officer, Sergeant Carter, is free. You mentioned a valuable trinket which you believe has been stolen? Would you care to give me further particulars?"

Mervyn now removed his hat and said that he would prefer to discuss the matter with the highest authority.

"Very good, sir," the constable replied and then, with a wink at Lucy he added, "Good morning, Lucinda. I hope your brother has recovered. We heard that he was in good form when the panda brought him back to Pollards last night."

He then called another constable to take his place at the counter and telephones, tapped on a door at the back of the office and went in.

"Now, Lucy," her father said. "There is no need for you to be nervous. I have a high opinion of our police force and, with my help we shall soon settle this disagreeable affair and I shall be able to get back to work."

"I'm not scared of the police, Dad. They were wonderful to Humf last night and I'm sure they'll be glad if we can help them. But I am afraid of that man who sold you the thing, and I want to see the panda policeman and tell him I'm sorry."

They were then invited into Sergeant Carter's office and Lucy sat in a comfortable chair by the window after shaking hands with a middle-aged man in uniform. Mervyn, sitting on the other side of the desk, made one attempt to gain control but was outclassed.

A constable sat at another desk taking notes as Mervyn repeated his story of the young man who sold him the snuff-box and produced the latter at the dramatic moment and passed it to the sergeant. After consulting a list the officer confirmed that what Mervyn had previously called a "trinket" was not on the list of articles already reported stolen, but that the police would like to keep it and would give Mervyn a receipt for it.

"I believe this to be genuine and valuable, Mr. Brown, and of course we'll make immediate enquiries. We have most of the facts now but you have not mentioned how much you gave this chap for the snuff-box."

Mervyn glanced at his daughter, and then to the sergeant.

"It was a trivial amount and I would prefer to mention it to you in private."

The sergeant nodded and turned to Lucy.

"We haven't much to ask you, Lucinda, and we are grateful for what you told Constable Harris last night when he brought your brother back to Pollards . . . No, my dear. There is no need for you to stand up . . ."

But Lucy was already standing by her father's chair with her hands behind her back and her chin held high.

"Thank you, but I can say it better standing up. If your constable is here I would like to speak to him, please. I told him a lie and I've been worrying about it ever since, and I want to tell him that I'm sorry."

Sergeant Carter smiled at her but spoke first to her father.

"I congratulate you on your daughter, Mr. Brown. Thank you, Lucinda. That was well spoken. P.C. Harris is out on duty but I will give him your message. You'll see him again one day. I'm sure you were listening to your father just now and you will remember that he told me the young man we want was seen by you and your brother in the castle grounds. You didn't tell the constable that you had seen him before because you wanted to tell your father first. We all understand this. Constable Harris believed that you had seen him before and told us why in his report. Forget this now, but remember, as you have been told at school, that the police are here to *help* people as well as to stop things going wrong. Now Lucy, this is the last question, but please think carefully before you answer. We have from you and your father a good description of this young man and you know why we want him. The question is this. When he saw you through the kitchen window of Pollards do you think he recognised you?"

"Yes, I do, sir."

"And the only time you had seen each other before was when he was with your father in the castle grounds? You mean that he knew you were the daughter of the man who had bought a valuable snuff-box from him, which almost certainly he had stolen?"

"I suppose so, sir."

"Good girl, Lucy. Thank you very much." Then he turned to Mervyn. "We believe this man is working for the woman artist, and was probably watching Pollards—or about to do so—when he heard Lucy calling for her brother. He is now aware that he has heen recognised by someone who knows he had the snuff-box . . . We have telephoned Mr. Strang, and although he doesn't think the young man stole anything, he agrees that the four youngsters are not safe in their camp so near the forest and out of sight of the house. Sorry to be dramatic about this, but we're going to search the forest with dogs, and our men won't want to be distracted by worrying about these children. Mr.

Strang offered to have them up closer to the house . . ."

"I agree, Sergeant," Mervyn interrupted. He had been silent for too long. "I have not yet met Mr. and Mrs. Strang, but I'm sure when they know the facts they will see the danger——"

"They do, Mr. Brown, and they are aware of the facts. By now the children have probably been told that they must strike camp. Lucy can be taken to join them in a few minutes by one of our chaps who is going to make further enquiries at Pollards."

"Excellent, Sergeant. I agree, and have an idea for an admirable compromise. Lucy, my dear, do you not think that the Hogbens would allow you all to camp in one of their fields until this matter is settled? Of course, that is the solution! Will you permit me to telephone from here, Sergeant, and then you will know where we shall all be."

The Sergeant lifted the receiver of his telephone and asked for Conways.

Lucy was now back on her chair and had no difficulty in hearing Mrs. Hogben's answer. She also heard the rest of an astonishing conversation which obviously fascinated the sergeant who had not met her father before. He began by saying the police had asked him to help them find a grey-haired woman hiker—and at mention of this unknown character, Lucy also heard Mrs. Hogben's snort of disgust—who had stolen Beau Nash's snuff-box and that she should tell her husband to take special care to lock up everything they had. He, Mervyn Brown, was in the police station now, and before Mrs. Hogben could answer he explained that Lucy was with him because she had a valuable clue; that Humf had been injured and that for various reasons the police thought the four children should leave the camp at Pollards because a gang of thieves were thought to be hiding in the forest.

When eventually Mrs. Hogben was able to speak, Lucy heard her say, "No real idea of what you're talking about, Mr. Brown. We're sick and tired of mad hikers and thieves, but of course the four kids can come over when they like. Plenty of places for them to camp here. Ask the Strangs to telephone me when they're ready and I'll come over in the Land-Rover—and don't think that means I haven't enough to do. That car of Strangs can only take two people and a dog . . . Give my love to your wife. Cheerio!"

"That is entirely satisfactory, Sergeant. The children will be at Conways this afternoon."

"Thank you, Mr. Brown. They'll give you a receipt for the snuff-box outside, and if you, Lucinda, will wait, we'll take you to Pollards in a few minutes . . . Goodbye, Mr. Brown, and thank you for your ready help."

When Lucy's father had gone, a woman police constable took her down to the canteen. They had coffee and a cheese roll and Lucy felt happier about her father, and almost lighthearted now that she had confessed why she hadn't told the truth last night to Constable Harris.

She was enjoying her second roll and thinking how envious Humf would be when she told him about this morning's adventure and her important interview, when another sergeant bustled in and came over to their table.

"Thanks for looking after Lucinda," he smiled at her companion. "Sorry, I've got to take her now as we're off to Pollards right away . . . And how's that comic young brother of yours, Lucy? Lucky we were in the forest yesterday. Bring what's left of your breakfast with you."

"You must be Sergeant Maycock," Lucy said as she

jumped up. "Thank you for rescuing Humf. He's crazy about your dog, Dandy. Is he coming with us?"

"More like we're going with him," the sergeant laughed. "That dog does everything except drive the car. Come and meet Dandy. I told my girl Betsy about your brother last night. She says she knows you by sight, but you're not in the same set or something . . . I can't make head nor tail of these big schools today, but I must say you all look well on whatever they teach you."

He led her into a special car park behind the police station, and instead of opening the door of one of the smart pandas or even one of the important looking cars with a blue lamp on the roof, he went to the back of an ordinary and well-used popular make of estate car. He unlocked the double doors and said something which Lucy didn't hear. Then out jumped the most beautiful alsatian dog she had ever seen. He looked up at his master, gently wagging his tail, and then the sergeant said, "Make a fuss of him, Lucy. Call him by name and help him to remember you."

She stroked the dog's head and put her arms round his neck and whispered, "Thank you for finding Humf, Dandy. Good dog, Dandy! Dandy is a lovely name for you. Don't ever forget us."

The dog moved his head so that he could lick her hand and his tail moved in appreciation of the affection in her voice.

"Take him round the car park, Lucinda. Just enough for him to stretch his legs. He'll go with you. I'm going to report that we're on our way."

Out of the side of his mouth he spoke again to the dog, and although Lucy couldn't hear what he said, Dandy undoubtedly understood and followed her round and then jumped into the back of the car.

The drive to Pollards did not take long. Lucy liked

Betsy's father and was almost sorry when they arrived because, as he drove, he told her many interesting things about the way police dogs are trained. She had already heard something of this from Humf, but having met Dandy herself now she was almost as fascinated. He told her that Dandy and he had worked together for over six years, and that dogs who were thought to be suitable came from kennels or private breeders, but were rarely accepted if they were over a year old. Then, with the officer chosen to be their handler, they went to a special training school together for thirteen weeks and that man and dog were taught to work together. Lucy longed to ask him what sort of lessons they did, but the sergeant was so keen to talk about his work that she didn't like to interrupt him. He explained that the dogs lived with their handler and his family, and although supposed to live out of doors in a kennel, older dogs in very cold weather lived indoors just as a pet dog would. When used for tracking, as Dandy and other dogs were going to search the forest this morning, each wore an easy-fitting harness at the end of a long nylon line. The sergeant said that the harder the ground the more difficult it was for a dog to follow a scent, and of course the fresher the scent the easier it was for him.

"A dog like Dandy can also find articles that a thief on the run throws away, and if nobody told you, Lucy, there are plenty of hiding places in the forest for a man on the run. We've found them before and that's why we think it's a good idea for you to move from Pollards . . . Nice people though, and here's Mr. Strang coming up the lane to meet you."

He stopped the car and as Lucy jumped out she heard Mr. Strang say, "Good morning, Sergeant. They telephoned to say that you were on your way and that you're going to search the forest for that young man.

You seem more worried than I am about him, but I agree about bringing the youngsters up from the edge of Deadman's Wood. I walked up to meet you because I've just had some interesting news. The bicycle used by the man you want was stolen from a chap who works half-days here for me with the turkeys. He lives about a mile away—you passed his cottage on the way now—and he had to walk here this morning in a very bad temper. Before I could tell him about our troubles yesterday, he said that he's found his bike thrown in a ditch just at the top of the lane and that the front brake was jammed and the wheel buckled or something. Thought you ought to know this. Obviously our red-headed visitor had a crash and deserted the machine which had been left outside Charlie's cottage . . . Pleased to see you again, Lucinda. All well here including your brother. They've started to break camp——"

"Sorry, sir," the sergeant interrupted, "but this news is important and with what we now know it's likely this chap has spent the night in the forest. I must report at once and I want the yard outside the kitchen window kept clear, please. I've got the dog here and although there's not much chance now of him picking up a scent after all this time, it will be more difficult if the youngsters trample all over it . . . See you later, Lucy. Thank you, sir."

This was a broad hint, so Mr. Strang and Lucy walked back to Pollards leaving the sergeant to his radio telephone.

"All right at home now, Lucinda?" Mr. Strang asked.

"It's all right now, and thank you and Mrs. Strang for being so kind to me. I can tell you now why I had to go and see my father at once."

She did so. Mr. Strang pressed her fingers, and as

they crossed the yard and heard the laughter of the others down at the camp he said, "That was brave of you, Lucinda. Nobody can be happy and live with a lie, but I think you will find one day that P.C. Harris knew you were unpleasantly concerned by his closer question about the blue jeans. I shouldn't say too much about it to the others. Mrs. Hogben is coming to fetch you all after an early picnic lunch and you can camp at Conways. We hope you will all come here after this trouble has been cleared up . . . Run along now and meet the others."

But the excitements of a day that had started so early for Lucy were not yet over. Peggy saw her first and ran to meet her.

"Everything O.K. at home, Lucy? You've heard the news that we've got to go?"

"It's all right now, Peg. Thanks for this morning. I've been to the police station with my dad about the red-headed man who was spying on us yesterday. I had to tell them about him, and as I thought I'd seen him before with my father I wanted to ask him first. I'll tell you all about it one day, but Betsy Maycock's dad is a sergeant and has just brought me back with Dandy. He's super."

She had to tell her story again to John and Humf. The former was not in a good mood because he thought it absurd to break camp just because a mad red-headed man was wanted by the police for questioning, but when Humf realised that he was actually within a few hundred yards of Dandy, and that the police were going to search the whole forest without his personal help, he nearly exploded.

"Of course the sergeant will want me. And Dandy too. I can walk can't I? I've got my wounds done. I'm not afraid of nadders. I'm not afraid of the forest or this stupid Deadman's part of it . . . It's your fault,

Lucy. Why didn't you tell the sergeant that he was to wait for me?"

They calmed him by suggesting going to the house and watching the yard through one of the windows to see whether Dandy could pick up the scent. This, they were in time to see, and even John forgot his ill-humour as he watched the dog, at the end of the nylon lead, nosing round the ground under the kitchen window. After a while he followed the old scent round the corner of the outhouse where Lucy had seen the tracks of the cycle tyres. Then they heard the sergeant's car start and guessed correctly that he had taken the dog up to where the bicycle had been found in the ditch, and they heard later that he had found the scent again without much trouble and led his handler into the forest.

Sadly they went back to the camp site and packed up. John recovered his good humour, teased Lucy, and remarked that the luckiest of them all was Mark who was soon off on a proper holiday. They discussed where they would camp at Conways, and before they started on their last journey up to the house they went to the "adder gate" and, standing still, they listened in vain for the bark of Dandy or one of the other dogs working the forest which would warn their handlers that they had found their man.

But there was no sound but the wind sighing in the treetops of Deadman's Wood and the faint hum of traffic on the main road a mile away. So they returned to the house and enjoyed Mrs. Strang's sandwiches in the garden. They had just decided to go and see the turkeys when Mrs. Hogben arrived in the Land-Rover.

"Sorry about all this trouble, my dears," she said as she got out. "I'll go and have a word with Mrs. Strang while you get your gear in the back and don't leave anything behind. All this shifting about seems nonsense to me, but you're welcome at Conways . . . Yes, Humf, my lad, I'm very sorry for you but you'll get over it . . ."

But Humf had the last and most important word on that important day. When they had thanked the Strangs and promised to come again, John asked his mother to drive a few miles further round and go back to Conways by the coast road.

"The police are working with their dogs from that side as well, and there's just a chance that we might see something happen, Mum. And Lucy and Humf haven't seen the tourist traffic in summer yet—although that's not really worth seeing I suppose. Anyway they haven't seen that side of the forest which comes right up to the road. And Humf might notice another police car which is one of the joys of his life after nadders."

So, as John had suggested, Lucy and Humf saw for the first time the endless stream of traffic along the main coast road through Sussex, into Kent to Dover. They were travelling slowly in a westward stream of traffic with some open pasture of the Downs on their left and the forest on the right of the road, when a stalled car on a hill slowed everything down. John and Peggy were on the front seat with their mother, while Lucy and Humf were in the back behind all the camping gear. As it was hot the roof was down, and both Lucy and Humf were leaning over the open side of the Land-Rover looking for any police activity on the forest side of the road. The east bound traffic was moving fairly fast while they were at a standstill, and suddenly Lucy saw, in a blue saloon car as it passed them, the man for whom the police were searching. He was sitting on the back seat on the driver's side behind a man and his wife who were obvious holiday makers. She had no doubt at all.

"Look, Humf!" she shouted as she pointed to the

man they had first seen in the castle grounds at Malling. "There he is! He was just putting on his dark specs. Did you see him?"

Humf nodded and yelled, "Yes, Lucy. That's him. We've got to find a telephone or a police car. I've got that car's number. That's what Dandy told us to do!"

6

Thursday: Jasper on the Run

NOT far from the coast road and the forest a small tidal river wanders down a sheltered valley called Greenhaven and finds the sea between the towering chalk cliffs. Mark Simson first took Lucy to Greenhaven, which is not far from Malling, because he was a keen birdwatcher, and because this valley is sheltered it is a refuge for many seabirds and, in a hard winter, for geese who fly south in search of warmer conditions.

On the eastern slope of the fields close to the mouth of the river there is a camping site and a rough car park, and throughout the summer months this is very popular. A few hours after the young Browns and Hogbens left Pollards, a girl of about twelve with two old-fashioned plaits strolled up the track which led from the beach between the river and the caravan site up to the main road. At her heels frisked a brown mongrel puppy and neither of them appeared to have a care in the world.

Away from most of the campers and close to the track, a woman was sitting on a canvas stool behind an easel and painting. The girl passed her as slowly as she dared because she knew it would be rude to look at the artist's picture although she wanted very much to do so. Although she did not get much encouragement from her busy parents, there was nothing which gave her more fun and pleasure at school than "Art." She sketched and painted whenever and wherever she could, and in her duffel bag which she had left with her mother on the beach was a sketch book. She had been trying to put on paper with a soft pencil and not much success the grace and beauty of the herring gulls wheeling and mewing above the cliffs.

So she walked very slowly, trying to think of a polite excuse for asking to see the picture. Out of the corner of her eye she noted that the woman was elderly and rather good-looking in a gypsy-like way. She had a gaily-coloured scarf over thick dark hair and big gold rings in her ears. She was looking at her work with half-closed eyes and with her head slightly on one side. A cigarette smouldered between her lips, but she didn't even look up until the puppy bounded up to her playfully and barked a friendly greeting.

This was the girl's chance.

"Come here *at once*, Nipper," she called. "How dare you? *Nipper!*" Then, "I'm so sorry he's bothered you. He's only a baby really, but his behaviour with strangers is better than it was. He's quite harmless."

The woman looked up and, to the girl's surprise, didn't seem to be particularly annoyed. She actually patted Nipper's head with the hand that wasn't holding a paint brush and said, "Silly little dog. I'm not going to play with you now," and then to Lucy, "Better put him on his lead, dear. He mustn't knock my easel over."

The girl pounced on the puppy and made him fast and then said shyly, "Thank you for not being cross with him, and please may I look at your painting? I love pictures and I'm not just being nosey."

"That's more than I can say for most people who pass me when I'm working. They don't even *ask* if they can look and there are some who would like to take my brushes and do it better than I can . . . Of course you may look, and not to worry about the little dog. I like dogs. Are you staying up in the camp? I don't think I've seen you about but I've only been here two days and I'm soon off on my travels again. What's your name, dear, and I wish you luck if you want to be an artist."

"It's Elizabeth Maycock, but everybody calls me Betsy. I live in Malling which is not far away, and because it's a lovely day and I've just broken up for the holidays my mother brought me here for a swim. We often come in the summer and the 'bus brings us to the top of this track . . . I like your picture very much. Do you mind if I ask whether you are a *real* artist? I mean do you paint for fun or because you can——"

Betsy was too shy to finish her question and the woman laughed at her.

"You mean can I sell what I paint? Strangely enough, Betsy, I can and do. I shall sell the painting of Greenhaven that you're looking at now to a publisher of picture postcards. I try to find a good view that other people will like to remember and paint it. As you live near here, perhaps you can tell me of some other places worth painting? Sit down beside me and keep that puppy from chewing up my tubes of paint . . . My name is Elizabeth too. Elizabeth Sandford and sometimes you will see it on a postcard and remember the old woman you met working in the sun at Greenhaven. I don't like staying too long in one place and I'm moving on tomorrow. I just hitch what I call my old wagon to the old car up there behind you and wander off somewhere else."

Betsy wasn't really sure that she liked the painting although she had politely admired it. There was rather a lot of blotchy colour in it and the scene didn't look much like Greenhaven as she looked down the river to the sea, but perhaps that didn't matter. Anyway Mrs. Sandford must have an interesting life going round in her caravan, and she was about to say so when she saw her mother standing on the top of the bank of shingle through which the river ran across the beach into the sea. She was waving and Betsy heard her calling her name. Nipper heard it too and began to struggle at the end of his lead.

"That's my mother calling," Betsy explained. "I expect the tide is low enough now for us to wade through the river where it's shallow and walk back over the cliffs. Thank you for showing me your picture and I'm sorry I must go now and haven't time to suggest some other places for you to paint . . . Why don't you come to Malling and paint the old castle? Lots of artists do . . . Goodbye. Say 'thank you,' Nipper."

"Goodbye, Betsy. Maybe I'll come to Malling one day and look out for you. What does your father do?"

"My dad is a policeman. A sergeant with a very special job . . . Goodbye."

She ran with Nipper trying to fight with his own lead and turned to wave to the gypsy-like Miss Sandford. But the artist didn't notice her as she had obviously finished work for the day and was folding up her easel and stool.

If Betsy had seen her face as she turned to trudge up the track towards her caravan, she would hardly have recognised the woman who had chatted to her in such a friendly way.

The path by which Miss Sandford's caravan was parked, wandered up the hill towards the coast road away from the main camp. The artist had deliberately avoided the other campers although she had been friendly enough when she met them at the camp shop. True, she did rather like dogs and got on well with children, but she was not a gossip. Nobody took much notice of her, and this pleased her.

Just before she reached her caravan she saw, on the brow of the hill where some cattle were grazing, a man running towards her. The path was not often used. Occasionally a worker from the farm, sometimes a couple hiking, or children exercising a dog came this way and she always passed the time of day with them. Once or twice a nice lad brought a big dog down this track, but few people came down the hill, and there was something about the way in which the man was running which disturbed her. He was stumbling and staggering now. Suddenly she realised who he was. The doors of both the caravan and her car were locked, and by the time she had dropped her painting gear to fumble for her keys the young man reached her. His lank, red hair was dark with sweat and so was his shirt. His blue jeans were torn and his face scratched and bleeding. He would never know what had happened to his black specs.

Before she could find her keys the man collapsed against the car with his head on his hands which were resting on the roof. As he struggled for breath, Miss Sandford looked at him with distaste.

"What is the matter with you, Jasper?" she said quietly. "I ordered you not to contact me personally unless I told you where we were to meet. Pull yourself together and stop making an exhibition of us both. Why have you come here?"

"You've got to hide me," he gasped. "Better still

you've to get me right away. Police are after me. They've got dogs . . . *Don't stand there staring. I tell you they've got dogs* . . . I was a fool ever to say I'd come in with you and now you must help me. Open your caravan and let me in and then you can drive us both off somewhere. Take me to Newhaven where I can get a boat to France. I'm through with you just as soon as you've got me clear."

Miss Sandford's expression did not change. She watched him calmly without speaking, and then walked over to the caravan, unlocked the door and then looked up the track down which he had come running a few minutes ago.

"Get in, Jasper, and try to behave with some dignity even if you are a coward. Sit on the bunk and when you've got your breath you can tell me exactly what has happened and why the police are after you. I don't encourage callers here but if anybody does come do your best to behave as if you were my nephew who has walked over the cliffs from Seaford to have a cup of tea with me. You'd heard that I was about here doing some painting."

She went over to the little stove and filled the kettle. Not until she had lit the gas ring did she turn and look at him shrewdly. He was still gasping for breath, and when he raised his shaking hands to his head, she realised that he really was in a panic, and indeed if the police were actually on his trail the situation was delicate. For once her judgment of an accomplice had been wrong. This young waster had no courage and not much sense, and somehow or other she must get rid of him before leaving the caravan site as she had already intended to do.

Jasper groped in his jeans for a crumpled packet of cigarettes.

"Gimme a match," he demanded. "And be quick

about it. And don't waste time messing about with cups of tea. You're in as much trouble as I am if only you knew it, so stop putting on these woman-artist airs and graces. I'm not such a fool as you think. I can see you've been trying to disguise yourself. You're wearing a wig or else you've dyed your hair. Probably both. Your clothes are different too, but that's not going to help you. You've got to get me out of the country quick, because if you don't I'm telling the police all I know about you—and that's more than you think I know, you silly old woman."

Miss Sandford turned back to the hissing kettle, and it was as well that Jasper did not see how her face changed at his threat. She did not answer until she had made some tea and poured him a cup. Then, "Drink that and calm down, Jasper. I don't think anybody will follow you here but possibly you were wise to come and find me. Tell me exactly what has happened and then we'll decide what to do for the best. Just remember that nothing would be more obvious than for me to drive off right now just as you've arrived. Take your time, tell me exactly what has happened, and then we'll see what we can do to help each other . . . But there is one thing I'm sure you should remember, Jasper. It isn't very sensible for us to threaten each other, is it? Now sit back and relax while I watch the path through the window. I shall see anybody coming so there'll be a chance for you to hide, and I can assure you that I shall let nobody in."

Jasper poured some hot tea in his saucer and thoughtfully stirred it with a dirty finger. He wasn't quite sure now whether he had been wise to come here. She had told him that in an emergency he should write to her addressed to the camp shop. He had met her several times in her caravan at different places along the coast, but he still wasn't sure whether she realised how he had already tricked her more than once. She must help him now, but if she was going to be difficult, he might have a chance later of stealing the keys of her car and driving off in it. How much did she know?

He looked up at her over the saucer, and as if she could read his thoughts she said quietly:

"Tell me everything, Jasper. Whatever we do now depends on me knowing everything that has happened and why the police should want to see you."

"O.K. then. As you say, we're in this together and, fact is, I've had a bit of bad luck. Since we met last week I've been having a good look round some of these old places in the country but there isn't much doing and as you know, this spying around is a tricky business and you can't be too careful. I was careful, but yesterday I was recognised by a kid—girl of about twelve—who had seen me with her father in Malling on Tuesday."

"But what was wrong with that, Jasper? I did advise you strongly to keep away from towns like Malling. What were you doing with this other man?"

Jasper lit another cigarette.

"Just give me time. I'm telling you, aren't I? We can't get on if you keep on butting in . . . I've got to go to a town sometime, haven't I? I'm still allowed to eat and drink and I was in a caff in Malling when the chap who runs it—proper crank he was—got into conversation and after a bit I realised he'd got something to sell. They've got an old ruin of a castle in Malling, and because he didn't want anybody to see what he'd got to offer he took me out there and where nobody could see us he offered me a dull looking old snuff-box which I knew wouldn't be any use to us so——"

"How did you know it wouldn't be any use, Jasper? Can you describe it?"

"Of course. It wasn't gold or silver and there weren't any jewels. Made of tortoiseshell or something dull."

"Really, Jasper? Had it by any chance got a painting on the lid?"

"Yes. Yes, I reckon it had. Very dull. Picture of some plump woman. Anyway, I'd just decided that he'd probably pinched it and I wasn't going to be caught that way. I mean, we don't want to be associated with stolen goods, do we?"

And with this stupid remark, he leered at her as if he had been very clever.

"No, Jasper. That would never do. Go on."

"Well, I'd just passed it back to this dim bloke when these two kids—yes, that's right, there were two. His kids. The girl had a young brother and they'd been up in the ruins somewhere watching us and I didn't like the idea of that so I cleared off——"

Miss Sandford, still looking innocent but a little bewildered, shrugged her shoulders, refilled his cup and then went back to the window.

"Get on with the story, Jasper. What about the police? Where were you yesterday and how did you get here?"

"I reckoned I was on a good thing yesterday. Found a nice, lonely little farm house over the other side of the big forest across the coast road. Elderly couple live there alone except for about a hundred turkeys. I kept an eye on them because the place looks smart and well kept and the couple sort of respectable and quite well off. Useful sort of possibility I reckoned. Might well have quite a few pieces worth your investigation. Good place for a picture too. They might well have fallen for your line of talk, and when they went out in their old car I was sure there would never be a better chance of a look round. There was a dog but that was no trouble. I can deal with dogs as you know. They'll always take a chunk of raw meat specially doctored with a little something which keeps them quiet for an hour. Did I tell you I always carry some round with me in a plastic bag but that bitch wolfed the last bit yesterday. Anyway they'd left the kitchen door on the latch—and I'd just gone in when I heard a kid shouting. I had time to look through one of the windows in the front and saw the girl I'd seen at the castle the day before running fast up to the house. I got out and hid in the yard where I'd parked a push bike I'd borrowed from a cottage on my way. The girl went in the house by the front door which must also have been unlocked and started yelling again for her brother, I suppose. After a bit all was quiet and I reckoned she'd gone out again by the front door so I went up to the kitchen window to have a look in. She was standing at the bottom of the stairs—yes, the stairs go up from the kitchen like in many farmhouses—and she recognised me. I didn't want that. Didn't want any words with her because she must have known the old couple, and there was the doped dog, too, so I got away quick on the bike and from then my luck was clean out. At the top of the lane I met the farmer and his wife coming back in the car. I knew they'd never seen me before, but the girl would tell them and there was the dog, you see."

He paused for breath and to see what effect his story was having on his patient listener. All that Miss Sandford did was to nod sympathetically and agree that, of course, there was the doped dog to account for.

"Go on, Jasper. What happened next? Where did you spend the night and did you notice whether this farm is on the telephone? I understand about the dog."

He was not looking so confident now.

"No. I was disturbed. Didn't notice a telephone. Place is a long way from the road. After I'd passed the returning car I had an accident with the bike. Front brake jammed or something. I was thrown off, so I chucked the thing in the ditch and reckoned I'd better keep out of the way for a bit. Spent the night in the forest. Wasn't too bad and I took my time finding a place to sleep."

"But why the panic, Jasper? What's all this about police dogs? Why should the police want you so badly? You've poisoned a dog and entered a house through a door that wasn't locked. Why should the police search the forest with dogs for somebody like you who has behaved like a fool? I think you're a liar, Jasper. *What else did you do in that house? What have you stolen?* Why do the police want you so urgently?"

He stood up and in a fit of childish temper flung his cup and saucer against the side of the caravan.

"Just listen to me," he shouted. "Don't you start on me now. I tell you they're after me and you've got to get me out. And I want food too. I'm starving. All this has happened because I look after your interests and because the girl recognised me. I heard the dogs after me this morning so I had to go careful. The main road goes along the south edge of the forest and I decided to thumb a lift and get to Dover. Get anywhere away from those dogs. It took a long time and I had to choose the right car but I got one in the end—silly old couple bumbling along about thirty. Anyway they stopped and I told them a yarn about my mother in hospital in Dover and he fell for it. I was just going to ask them for food when we got in a traffic jam and then the worst happened. Coming the other way in a Land-Rover were those two kids again. They recognised me. I know they did and sooner or later there would be a police call out for that car."

Miss Sandford stooped to pick up the broken fragments of crockery and made no comment until she had carefully put the pieces in a litter bin under the small sink. Then she returned to the window and looked again up the track.

"So the two children who saw you with their father in Malling recognised you? And you, in a silly panic jumped out of the car which would have put you down in Folkestone or Dover by now, and came rushing down here with the chance of getting us both into trouble. And you dare to threaten me, Jasper, forgetting what I have already paid you and forgetting that all I want from you is information. I have never asked you to steal for me, but I am now certain that you have been stealing for yourself and that's why you're in a panic—and if the police are after you it's because they know you've been stealing. You're a fool because you think I'm going to believe your story. Even if those children did recognise you an hour ago, they're not likely to tell the police just because you were staring through a kitchen window."

"There was the dog. They'd find her doped. Even if the girl didn't the farmer would, and if they thought I'd been in the house they'd tell the police wouldn't they?"

"They might, Jasper, but you're very frightened and if you took nothing from the house they can't prove anything, can they? And these two children wouldn't be likely to take the number of your car when they were travelling in the opposite direction. And why should you be so worried because they saw you in Malling? You say that the owner of the café was trying to sell you a stolen snuff-box. He's the man the police want, surely. Not you. I think you're a liar, Jasper, and before you get out of here for good you're going to tell me the truth. And not only are you a liar but——"

During all this conversation Miss Sandford had never raised her voice, so the sudden deep bark of a large dog somewhere outside was a dramatic interruption. Jasper jumped up and she looked quickly through the window and then stood in front of it so that he could not see out.

"You've got to save me," Jasper whimpered. "I told you they were after me. Let me hide in here. Go out and keep them off. I'll do anything for you. I swear I will. Just save me now. That's all I ask . . ."

The dog barked again. Much nearer this time, but Miss Sandford neither lost her nerve nor raised her voice.

"I'll tell you what I'm going to do, Jasper, when I've finished telling you what I think of you. We've just got time before the dog stops at this caravan and we must understand each other quickly. I believe you've been stealing from houses when you should only have been investigating for me. I am now sure that before I moved on to east Sussex you stole from this caravan. You may well have been fool enough to try and sell what you stole in towns like Malling to innocent people. It is also possible that when you believed the police were on your trail that you hid what you hadn't sold in the forest. Because of your stupid blundering we now have to move from here sooner than I had intended. Or I must move. I'm not sure of you yet . . . Now, Jasper. The dog is within twenty yards. Listen."

The young man hid his face in his hands as the dog barked again.

"Are you going to do as I tell you, Jasper? Precisely what I tell you without any argument? If you don't I shall let the dog in here and lock you in with him. And remember that there is nothing you can do to me. Last week I was an innocent hiker exploring another part of this delightful county, and now I'm an innocent artist painting another part of Sussex and can prove it. There's nothing in this caravan of particular value if it is searched. The Post Office works for me, Jasper. Parcels can be sent anywhere without any questions being asked provided you put stamps on them, you silly little man. Nobody will believe a word you say if you try to betray me."

The dog was growling outside now and Jasper shrank back on the bunk when he heard first the scratching of the animal's claws on the door and then its triumphant bark.

"Keep it out! Keep it out," he whimpered. "I'll do anything."

Miss Sandford turned her face away so that he couldn't see her smile. There was no need to tell him that the big dog outside belonged to a family of campers down by the beach—a dog she liked and had fussed over and given tit-bits to from time to time. He was only asking for more.

7

Thursday: News for the Police

"STOP! Please stop, Mrs. Hogben!" Humf shouted from the back of the Land Rover. "The man in the back of that car is wanted by the police. Honest, he is! Please stop somewhere—specially at a telephone box. Or if you see a policeman or a panda car."

"Be quiet, boy!" Mrs. Hogben retorted. "Sit down and stop making an exhibition of yourself. I can't stop now as there are about a hundred cars on my tail and five hundred in front of us in this traffic block. Keep the child quiet, Lucy, there's a good girl."

Humf, with tears of anger in his eyes, was forced down on his knees.

"Write it down, one of you," he pleaded. "I've got the number. Listen, John. Find a pencil in case I forget . . . JAP 452 D . . . JAP 452 D. It's an old Morris 1100 saloon. Blue. And it's JAP 452 D. We've got to remember it. The red-headed chap the police want was in that car. He's the man Lucy saw nosing round Pollards. What did I say it was? JAP what? Dandy told us when he came to our school that we could help him if we remembered the numbers of cars. None of you seem to understand what this means to me. We've just got to help the police.

John turned round from the front seat beside his mother and tried to comfort him.

"O.K. Humf. Pipe down. We know you saw him and we'll tell the police as soon as we can. Mother can't stop now in all this traffic. You as sure as Humf, Lucy?"

"Yes, I am. I'll never forget that man and I was the first to see him. He was just putting on his dark specs and perhaps he didn't recognise us . . . I can't be sure because they were going fairly fast but Humf has been the clever one. He's got the number—JAP 452 D . . . Please ask your mother to take us straight to the police station at Malling, John. That would be quicker than trying to find a phone box on this main road."

Peggy, who so far had said nothing, glanced at her mother after writing the car number on a scrap of paper. Mrs. Hogben was looking annoyed and Peggy recognised the signs only too well. First she knew that Thursday was Mrs. Hogben's baking day and she didn't like her household plans upset. Peggy also guessed that she hadn't been too pleased about coming over to Pollards to fetch them all, and was also annoyed by Humf's tearful insistence that she must stop the car. So she was not really surprised when her mother, without taking her eyes from the road, spoke loudly and firmly.

"Listen all of you. I am not going to stop again even if we do pass a telephone box. Will you please stop fussing and chattering until we get to Conways. I've heard everything you've been saying, Humphrey, and when we get home in about five minutes I will listen to you again. Now, if you please, you will all keep quiet. I have had a busy day and I want to get back to my oven."

"If I may just speak once more," Humf pleaded quietly. "Just once, please Mrs. Hogben. If you should just happen to see a panda car coming along the road —it's a pale blue car with white doors and a white strip on the roof. If you should just happen to notice one, would you please flash your lights at him so that he stops . . . An' if he does stop, Mrs. Hogben, maybe you wouldn't mind stopping too so that I could report like Dandy told me to do."

The four children glanced at each other in a silence which was broken only by the roar of traffic now streaming by in each direction. Then they looked expectantly at Mrs. Hogben who suddenly relaxed and smiled at Humf in the driving mirror.

"Bless the boy," she laughed. "You're a real caution and no mistake. You'll never lie down, will you? Yes, Humphrey. If I meet a panda I'll flash my lights and you can take over, but when we get home to Conways I'm going to do the talking."

And so she did. When she drove into the farmyard ten minutes later, Humf was the first to jump out and open the driver's door for her. Her smile was grim as she thanked him and said, "Now if you please you will listen to me. I am tired of all this talk and fuss about grey-haired women artists who are thieves, and strangers nosing round our houses. The Hogbens are people who keep themselves to themselves and get on with the job. We're friendly to all and we've nothing against the police, but we don't want our children mixed up in all these goings on. Only this morning I was talking to Mr. Hogben about it and he agrees that John and Peggy are to keep out of this business. And Lucinda, it's not for us to interfere with what your parents think, but while you're at Conways—and you're always welcome—we must ask you the same . . . Now, don't look at me like that, Humphrey. You got lost yesterday and everybody for miles round was worried and fussing about you. You can set up your camp here, but it seems to me that the safest place for all of you will be on the front lawn where we can keep an eye on you and not even the police can interfere."

"You can't really mean that, Mum," Peggy protested. "Dad would never let us have a fire on the lawn and a camp isn't a camp without a fire. We don't think you're being fair about this. Of course we'll be careful about a fire on the farm, and we won't go off anywhere without telling you but——"

Before her mother could answer Lucy stepped forward and with her hands behind her back—she always stood like this when she had something special to say—and spoke out firmly:

"We're very sorry, Mrs. Hogben, but really everything that has happened and has upset you and made everything rather troublesome for you and Mr. Strang is *our* fault. I mean the Brown family's fault. I wanted to tell you all exactly how we got mixed up with this horrible young man so that you understand better why we're so upset. Now I think we've become rather a nuisance to you, and if we haven't thanked you *very* much for fetching us from Pollards, I do now and so does Humf. What I want to say is that if we really are a nuisance Humf an' me can easily walk back to Malling or catch a bus and go to the Police Station before we go home to the *Blackbirds*. Of course we should appreciate it very much if we could use the telephone here before we start on our journey."

This was very clever of Lucy who wasn't even trying to be. Truth was that she was very tired after the strain of the interviews with her father and the police and the excitements of the day. Mrs. Hogben looked at her shrewdly and suddenly all her ill-humour vanished again and she stepped forward and put her arm round Lucy's shoulders.

"You're a good girl, Lucinda, and I'm sorry if I was short with you. Stay here as long as your parents will let you, and if this young detective wants to go and telephone the Police Station you'd better go with him. John and Peggy had best go up the fields and find their father and tell him what's happened and ask where you can camp."

Almost before she had finished speaking, Humf was running into the house. Lucy smiled her thanks at the Hogbens and followed her brother.

"That was good, Lucy," he said as he lifted the receiver. "Jolly good. Now we have to dial 999 and when I tell the right chap they'll send radio messages absolutely flashing out to those police cars and to Sergeant Maycock who will tell Dandy, and to all the chaps on those motor bikes and they'll find old ginger-whiskers . . . Hello there! I want the police absolutely vital and urgent. Is that you? The police I mean. Good! Then just you listen——"

"Ask to speak to Sergeant Carter," Lucy hissed in his disengaged ear. "He's the man I saw with Dad this morning. He's nice. He'll do everything."

Humf nodded violently.

"I have vital news for Sergeant Carter," he said firmly. "My name is Humphrey Mervyn Brown of the *Four & Twenty Blackbirds* with which you are acquainted. Will you kindly inform him that he saw my father and sister this morning and that I have the number of the car in which the man he is looking for is escaping in——"

Here he paused for breath and so, apparently, did the switchboard operator in the Police Station. Lucy, with her ear pressed to the other side of the ear-piece of the receiver, realised that her brother was shaking with excitement. Suddenly he was through and Lucy heard the Sergeant's voice.

"Good morning, Humphrey. Yes, I know who you are. Yes, I'm listening. Tell me as quickly as you can where you are and what you have to tell us."

Humf gulped and drew a deep breath.

"Sir Sergeant," he began. "I am at Conways Farm and I was telling you what we know because Dandy told us to remember car numbers of the car——"

"Yes, Humphrey. You're right. Dandy tells all boys and girls that. What is the number of the car you have seen, where was it and which way was it going and how long ago?"

"Tell him the number first in case we forget it," Lucy whispered. "Shall I tell him?"

Humf shook his head violently.

"Sir! The number is JAP 452 D and it's a blue Morris 1100. It was on the coast road and going Eastbourne way and we were in Mrs. Hogben's Land Rover going back to Conways the other way and we got stuck in a traffic jam if you know what I mean. And that's when we saw him!"

"I know, Humphrey. Go on," said the patient voice. "I've got the number."

"Well, Sir. That red-headed man who sold something to our dad and who was nosing round Pollards Farm where Lucy saw him yesterday, was in the back of this car and we think he'd got a free lift."

"How long ago, Humphrey?"

"Half an hour. Not more," Lucy hissed and Humf reported this.

"I thought you ought to know all this, Sergeant, and I hope I've done right in reporting it. I'd like Sergeant Maycock and Dandy to know that it's me because Dandy rescued me from the forest and the nadders."

"All concerned shall be informed, Humphrey. You have done well and the Sussex Constabulary is proud of you. We mustn't waste more time now but will you and your sister kindly wait at Conways until somebody comes to interview you . . . Goodbye Humphrey and give my love to Lucinda."

"Did you hear that?" Humf gasped as he replaced the receiver. "He sent you his love. He must be soppy. Did I do all right, Lucy? I can tell you that it's a real strain working with the police."

"Yes, Humf, it must be and I'd like to know where you'd be without me. I was the one who spotted Red-whiskers not you. And you forgot to tell my friend Sergeant Carter that the man they want may have recognised us . . . Hullo, Peg. Detective Insector Humf Brown has done his stuff and the police are following his advice. Has John gone to find your dad? I'd like to tell you all now why I had to go off early this morning by myself to see my father. I specially want you to know, Peg, because you didn't nag at me this morning when I was very unhappy. And I'd like to tell your parents too."

Peggy was liking Lucy better every time they met, and sometimes she felt mean because she hadn't been particularly kind to her at first. And she was still rather jealous of her friendship with Mark.

"You don't have to tell us, Lucy. Not if it's private to your family. Mum would understand and anyway we shan't get my father in the house for hours. Come in the kitchen then. Tea will be ready and John back soon . . . What about you, Humf? You're looking smug. Are you pleased with yourself?"

"Yes, Peg, I am . . . Just in two days I've been forced by my friends to chop wood and lug pails of water. I've been lost in the forest and practically starved and nearly attacked by fierce nadders. I've been utterly unconscious for hours and rescued by the most super police dog in the world . . . And I've been dragged back to life in a nospital and after all that I'm working with the police. I've been detecting and they know now what I can do for them. And now you ask me whether I'm pleased with myself. Can't you see that I'm so utterly weary that I can hardly stand? I would like to sit down in your kitchen for a very long time . . . What does smug mean anyway?"

The two girls led him with faltering steps into the kitchen and lowered him into a chair.

"He's exhausted, Mum," Peggy explained. "He says he's starving and I think he's joined the police . . . Good! Here's John. While we're having our tea Lucy has got something special to tell us."

John grinned cheerfully at the exhausted Humf who was rather disappointed because his hero didn't ask him any questions about his conversation with the police. All he said was, "Dad won't be down for a bit and said not to wait. What's Lucy got to tell us? You're looking very solemn, ducky. What's wrong?"

Lucy was getting used to making confessions but this one wasn't so difficult as the last. The Hogbens were her friends and as she looked round the room she had grown to love, she lost her shyness and told them how Humf and she had seen their father with the red-headed man in the castle grounds and watched him buy something from him and put it in his pocket.

"I didn't know then what it was," she went on. "I didn't know until this morning and it was awful of me because Dad said it was a secret present for my mother's birthday and we weren't to say anything about it. Then, you see, the man who was nosing round Pollards and who poisoned Mr. Strang's dog recognised me, just as I knew him, when he stared at me through the kitchen window. The really awful thing was when the police came and told us that they wanted to question this man because he was suspected of stealing precious things from lonely houses and farms. When that nice policeman asked me if I had seen the man before, I didn't own up and admit I'd seen him with my father. I was a coward——"

"Are you sure of that, Lucy dear?" Mrs. Hogben interrupted quietly. She was sitting in her favourite rocking chair while the four children were round the table. She looked at Lucy over the spectacles she used for reading and knitting and put the latter down in her lap.

"Are you sure you were a coward? I don't think so. You didn't own up to seeing the man before because you didn't know whether your father knew that he had bought something from a suspected thief. Wasn't that it? You didn't know what he had bought, did you? When I came to fetch you from the *Blackbirds* the other day a policeman was there talking about a woman hiker, wasn't he? He warned me and asked your mother to look out for her and I told him there were more important things for the police to be worrying about. But he didn't mention a young man, did he?"

Lucy shook her head but before she could continue her story John interrupted.

"I bet your father was surprised to see you. Did he show you the treasure after you'd explained why you'd come so bright and early in the morning? And why don't you tell us what it was? I can't stand the suspense, Lucy."

Lucy smiled at him.

"I've seen it. I've had it in my hands although we took it to the police as soon as Dad realised that it might have been stolen. We went to see the head man, another nice sergeant and Humf spoke to him on the telephone just now. He told us it was very valuable but nobody had reported that it was missing so we don't know for certain that it was stolen."

"Will you tell us what this precious treasure looks like? Peggy besought her. "You keep on talking about it but you don't say what it was. Was it some super sparkling jewellery?"

"No, of course it wasn't. I'm trying to tell you that it was a dull-looking snuff-box made of some dark stuff. Tortoiseshell, I think Dad said it was. It was round, and on the lid was a lovely little painting of a woman and that was the only nice thing about it. I couldn't understand why it was so valuable and I could see that my mother wasn't very excited about it either. I don't think she really minded about it going to the police. Of course she was thrilled that my father had thought of something so rare for her birthday, but she said that she didn't take snuff and hadn't any valuable jewels to put in it, which I thought was rather funny."

Nobody laughed and when Lucy looked round at the others she realised that John and Peggy were staring at their mother who had taken off her spectacles and was watching her with a puzzled expression on her kind face.

"Your father telephoned me from the police station, Lucy, and talked excitedly about a snuff-box that had belonged to Beau Brummel at Bath, but he was so excited and what with all this talk of women hikers and the fuss, fuss, fuss with the police and I'd got something in the oven, I didn't take too much notice except to say you might as well all come over here to camp for a bit. But Lucinda dear, what you have been telling us about this young man everybody is after has reminded me of something. I didn't see him when you were making so much noise in the Land-Rover, but will you describe him again to me very carefully. I've an idea that I might have seen him myself recently."

Two Hogbens and two Browns stared at her in silent astonishment. Then Humf said excitedly, "But Mrs. Hogben, all the police and Dandy are looking for him an' I've promised to help them and if you've seen him then——"

"That will do, Humphrey," Mrs. Hogben said sharply. "I asked your sister to speak. Now, Lucy."

So once again Lucy described the man who, in a few days, had done so much to upset their lives. To her surprise it was soon obvious that Mrs. Hogben had seen him. She put down her knitting and watched Lucy carefully while she was speaking and when she had finished she smiled triumphantly.

"That is a very good description of the young man who came here the other afternoon. What a coincidence! I must say I didn't care for him at all and, of course, in the end I sent him packing . . ."

"But, Mum," John? almost shouted as they crowded round her. "Why didn't you tell somebody before? Why did he come here? And when?"

"Oh dear, I do wish all you young people wouldn't get so excited. I'll try to tell you exactly what happened. Your father will probably remember that I told him about it when he came in late for his tea . . . And that reminds me, Peggy, dear. Put the kettle on again because he'll be here soon and he does like a freshly-made pot of tea and hates being kept waiting . . . There's a good girl . . . Don't glare at me like that, John. There's not really much to tell you . . . Yes, of course. It was last Monday at about this time. I was alone here and this young man came to the back door. He was quite respectful and asked if your father was in as he was looking for some spare-time farm work. I didn't think he'd be any good but supposed that Mr. Hogben should see him. He was scruffy and not very clean and when I told him I didn't think there were any jobs going, he asked where your father was, and when I said he might be in the farmyard or up in the fields he asked if he could wait or go and find him. I can't remember now why I went myself round to the cowsheds to see if he was about. He wasn't there and I just walked a little way up the fields—couldn't have been more than ten minutes—and as I couldn't see him I gave up and came back. The young chap was leaning against the barn as if his knees wouldn't hold him up and smoking like a chimney. I told him there was nothing doing and he slouched off without speaking . . . Funny about that snuff-box though, Lucy. We've got one somewhere. It was my grandfather's or great-grandfather's. It's not only the Hogbens are Sussex folk—my own people were downland farmers too. You remember that little box, don't you, Peg? You used to play with it when you were a baby."

"Better go and see if it's still in your dressing table drawer, Mum," Peggy laughed. "You'll look silly if Lucy's nasty young man stole it when you were up in the fields and then sold it to Mr. Brown. I'd forgotten all about it."

Mrs. Hogben looked uneasy.

"Don't be silly, Peggy love. I wasn't out of the house ten minutes. Your father will be here in a minute, but you might just run upstairs and check that our box is there safe and sound. You know where I keep it. Left hand drawer of the dressing table."

Peggy was some time upstairs and when Mr. Hogben came breezing in Lucy slipped out of the room and ran up to find her friend. She stood on the landing and called her name, and when Peggy came out of her parents bedroom she knew at once that she couldn't find the snuff-box.

"It's not there, Lucy. I've searched everywhere and I can't think what my dad will say when he knows that Mum left the door open and the man could nip into the house."

"And I can't think what mine will say when he realises the beastly little thing which he wanted to give my mother on Saturday really belongs to yours . . . I didn't really mean that it's a horrid thing, Peg. I didn't really think it was very beautiful but lots of old things aren't. I'm so sorry about all this because it's upset the start to the holidays. That's what I meant was beastly about it . . . Has anything else been stolen?"

Peggy shook her head as she closed the door behind her.

"I shouldn't think so. Mum doesn't notice much about her personal things. She told us once that she didn't think they were important and sometimes I think she's right. She doesn't worry about anything much except looking after us . . . Come on. We'd better go and break the news. Thanks for coming up, Lucy."

Humf was waiting for them at the bottom of the stairs.

"I bet it's gone," he hissed. "You can't fool me, Peggy. When you didn't come down with it I knew what had happened. Your dad is having his tea and Mrs. Hogben and John are trying to tell him what all the fuss is about. I don't think he's in a very good temper so it might be better if Lucy an' me went for a walk round the farmyard. I reckon my friends will be here soon and I'd like to be the first to welcome them . . . The police, I mean."

Peggy nodded. "O.K. then. Don't go too far away. Dad will be more angry about the man getting into the house than about the old snuff-box. Soon as we've got over this we'll fix where we're going to camp tonight . . . Cheerio."

So the Browns went out into the sunshine and sat on the farmyard gate. Bob, the Hogbens old dog was sitting outside his kennel and thumped his tail in greeting as they passed.

"That's funny, Humf. Mrs. Hogben never said anything about Bob who would have been certain to bark at our man when he arrived."

"He's always chained up, isn't he? If he'd made a row when Mrs. Hogben left the house, old red-whiskers might have chucked him some poisoned meat. Maybe there wasn't any need to and he just slipped into the house as soon as he saw her going up the fields . . . I wonder what's happened to him, Lucy? I wouldn't tell the others but I'm feeling a bit exhausted. It would be a nice change if nothing happened for a bit, wouldn't it?"

Lucy nodded. Everything was suddenly rather peaceful. The evening sunshine was glowing on the flint walls of the old farmhouse and the shadows of the big elms were lengthening across the yard. In the cowsheds one of Mr. Hogben's men was whistling melodiously, and there was a warm summer smell so different from the thick petrol fumes of the city in the midlands which they had left only six months ago.

"Do you ever remember Midchester, Humf?

Sometimes I can hardly believe we're here. They're all so nice to us, aren't they?"

Her brother looked up at a cloud of starlings circling and wheeling above the tree tops. He knew now that starlings in their hundreds returned to their special roosting places every evening. Mark had told them.

"Yes, they're O.K. Lucy. I was just wondering what our dad will say when he hears what's happened. And what will he tell Mother?"

Before Lucy could answer they heard the sound of an approaching car. Humf jumped to the ground and ran into the lane. Then he turned excitedly.

"It's the police, Lucy. It's a panda. Get down and open the gate and I'll see them in."

He held up his hand in warning and turned to Lucy and laughed excitedly as the driver recognised him and sounded his siren. As the gate swung back and the blue and white car drove slowly into the yard, Lucy recognised Constable Harris who had been so quick to guess that she had seen the man with the red whiskers before. She heard the Hogbens' Bob bark a warning and then felt herself colouring as the constable smiled at her before getting out of the car.

"Hullo, Lucy. Nice to see you again. I got your message this morning, thank you. Not to worry any more . . . And here's the young adder hunter. What's your news, son?"

Humf told him about the missing snuff-box in a few sentences without any full stops!

"Is that so? You two come along with me and talk to Mrs. Hogben. Robert will stay in the car just to pass on that bit of news."

P.C. Pinder winked at Humf who was standing on one leg with excitement.

"Have you got that man yet?" he shouted. "The

man I saw in the car the number of which I jolly well got for you?"

"The car was stopped just outside Rye, son, thanks to you. Nice couple they were. They confirmed that the chap we want thumbed a lift about a mile back along the road before you spotted him. Said he must get to Dover to see his mother in hospital. He jumped out of the car without a thankyou soon after you spotted him but we haven't found him yet. But we shall . . . Run in and tell the Hogbens we've arrived, will you?"

Humf, the police messenger, sped on winged feet to do his bidding and Lucy found herself walking more slowly with P.C. Harris.

"Smart chap your young brother, Lucy. Doesn't seem much wrong with his foot today. We thought we would come and have a chat with Mrs. Hogben and see what you were all up to. Does she really admit that she left the door of this house unlocked when she left that young chap outside? No wonder we're kept so busy."

Lucy didn't say anything. She was suddenly tired and wanted to go home. For the first time during the last few hectic days she felt sorry for the man the police were hunting and she wished it was all over and they were back where they started on the first day of the holidays.

When she led the constable into the kitchen Mr. Hogben, rather red in face, was standing with his legs apart in front of the great fireplace. He looked annoyed and Peggy and John rather subdued. Humf was sitting on the edge of a chair and swinging his legs.

"Good afternoon, Constable," the farmer said briskly. "I've just heard the story. My wife is upstairs searching the bedroom to see if anything else has been stolen. I understand her snuff-box is in your possession."

"We shall ask Mrs. Hogben to identify it, sir. You will have heard that it was bought by Mr. Brown from the young man we're anxious to interview. I'm sorry to bother you all again but I won't keep you long . . . Good afternoon, Mrs. Hogben. Any signs of anything else being stolen? You know that we have what is almost certainly your snuff-box safe and sound . . . Nothing else? Good."

Mrs. Hogben sat herself down firmly at the head of the table. Lucy looked across at Peggy and saw that her friend was trying to smother a smile. She guessed correctly that the farmer's wife was now going to dramatise the situation as her father would have done.

"Sit down, young man. Sit down. I've had a very tiring day and if you did but know it the work of a farmer's wife is never done! And you're the young man who came to the *Blackbirds* in Malling t'other day when I was talking to my friend Mrs. Brown. Of course you are. You're young Bill Harris and I knew your mother before you were born."

"You told me so before, madam. I was telling you about a woman with short grey hair who has been hiking about the country and doing a bit of painting. I want to ask you again whether you've seen such a woman and to ask you to telephone us immediately if you do."

"I'm more likely to chase her off the premises with a broom," Mrs. Hogben said grimly. "I know I've been made a fool of by that scruffy young man, but Mr. Hogben and I want to know where this business is going to stop. We're both busy. We can't always lock all the doors and windows every time I cross the farmyard. What are the police for is what we want to know . . . ?"

"Now, now, my dear. Take it easy," the farmer said and then turned to the constable. "What we want to know, young man, is whether there is a connection between the man who had the nerve to walk upstairs and pinch that snuff-box and the woman you keep telling us about?"

"Yes, sir. We believe he was working for her or with her and when we find him he may well lead us to her. For the moment we've lost touch with both of them but the man cannot be far away and a warning has gone out to all motorists about giving him a lift. And until he is found, Sergeant Carter feels it might be wiser if these young people—particularly the Browns—were just extra careful. Better not to camp out, he feels. The man we want to talk to knows that they have recognised him more than once. We don't know anything about him, but people on the run are often dangerous and if it's all the same to you we'd like to take these two back to Malling . . . There's only one other question I'd like to ask, Mrs. Hogben. What about your old dog, madam? He barked when we drove into the farmyard just now. Did he warn you when the man came to your door the other day?"

"Come to think of it I don't believe he did. He's getting old but he's still a good watch dog. I was upstairs when you arrived but I heard him then."

Lucy explained what had happened to the Strang's dog and then Humf, who had been unnaturally silent suddenly spoke in a loud voice to the constable.

"What I want to say is very, very vital. First I want to ask what has happened to my friend Dandy. Is he working all the time at finding old Redwhiskers?"

"Yes, son. I'm sure he is. You know his handler, Sergeant Maycock, don't you, and he'll be looking after Dandy as he always does but I don't suppose they're searching the forest now—not after that chap got a lift. And even police dogs must rest some time."

"Quite so," Humf agreed. "Police dogs must rest of

course. Do you think that Sergeant Maycock thinks that the chap might have gone back into the forest to hide after getting out of the car—just because everybody else will think he's got another lift, if you know what I mean?"

P.C. Harris acknowledged that he did know what Humf meant and he expected that his colleagues on the job had thought of everything.

"I expect they have," Humf agreed, "but I should like to offer my services to the police now and specially to Dandy. I reckon I could help him do some tracking. My father says it's never too early to start thinking about a career and I'm ready now to begin learning."

To his credit P.C. Harris did not smile.

"Thank you, Humphrey. Your offer will be conveyed to the correct quarters but just for a few days it would be better if you all got on with your holiday. We shall certainly ask for your help if we need it." Then he turned to the farmer:

"We know you're busy, sir—and you too, Mrs. Hogben. But I must ask you to look out for this chap and to lock your doors and windows if the house is left. And keep an eye on your barns and for any strangers and let us know at once if you're suspicious . . . Now may I take these two home?"

Mr. Hogben relaxed and smiled at them all.

"That's the best idea. Come back here and camp when you want to. Always welcome, but I'll be harvesting next week and John will be helping me. We'll do what you ask, Constable. I don't like this sort of thing any more than you do, but woe-betide that young thief if my missus catches him. He'd rather be locked up and much safer. And don't look so down-hearted, Peg. You've hardly started your holidays yet and there's plenty of time for camping out. Sorry you had that bit of trouble at Pollards. I'll have a word on the telephone with Strang this evening and tell him what's happened . . . Cheerio, and thanks for your help."

John and Peggy came out into the yard to say 'Goodbye' to the Browns.

"Please don't start for a minute," Lucy said to the two policemen as she leaned from the window for a last word with her friends. "I've got a wonderful idea, Peg. I told you that Saturday is my mother's birthday and Dad had an idea that we might take her in the evening to Smuggler's Cove for a barbecue . . .Will you two come if we do have a party like that? And if it's really a good place p'raps we could camp there next week if this horrid business is cleared up. Will you come if we ask you?"

"That's O.K. isn't it, Peg?" John agreed. "If your parents don't mind I'm sure ours won't. Mum will soon get over the snuff-box being pinched from under her nose and your father can make her a presentation of it if the police will let him have it. Smugglers Cove isn't too bad but it may be a bit crowded now in the holiday season. Lots of caravan campers from Greenhaven go down there but we can risk that and if the tide is right we can swim."

Peggy nodded enthusiastically and offered to bring some food so that Mrs. Brown wouldn't have to do any extra cooking, and then the panda drove out of the farmyard.

Within three minutes Humf was asleep in the back of the car. Lucy wasn't surprised because this often happened when he was excited and she knew that he would wake up full of enthusiasm before they got home.

P.C. Harris looked over his shoulder and smiled at Lucy.

"That brother of yours is dead keen isn't he, Lucy?"

"Yes he is. He says he's going to be a policeman and have a dog like Dandy. He'll go on fussing about Dandy all the holidays."

"Why don't you invite him to your party then? You know Betsy, don't you? She's at your school. Ask her to arrange a meeting with her father. She'll talk to him for you. Police dogs have fun sometimes as well as work. So do policemen for that matter."

"Thank you very much," Lucy smiled. "You've given me a wonderful idea."

8

Saturday: Happy Birthday

LUCY woke early on the morning of her mother's birthday. As usual, sparrows were scuffling in the gutters above her dormer window, and as she turned over and clasped her hands behind her head she heard the church clock strike six. As she opened her eyes, she remembered blissfully that today was special. No school, and still too early to wake her brother and take their parcels and greetings into their parents' room.

Lucy loved her little room with the steeply sloping ceilings. It had taken her weeks after they had moved in to remember that she must never sit up in bed suddenly. It was safer to roll out and then walk to the window and sniff the wind that so often blew up the valley from the south-west bringing with it the faint smell of the sea. She did this every morning when she wasn't fighting the usual battle against time, but six was too early to wake anybody, although she knew that she wouldn't sleep again now. There was too much to remember. Too much to hope for. Too many exciting things to happen today.

A patch of pale sunlight on the dingy ceiling promised well. As usual, it showed up the wavy crack that always reminded her of a river winding its way to the sea. Like the muddy, tidal river that slid under the bridge at the bottom of Malling Hill; the river which reached the sea at Greenhaven, cradled in the hills where the wild geese sheltered in the winter. The valley Mark had shown her because he wanted to share with her his enthusiasm for wild birds.

She smiled as she thought of Mark and of how she had met him in the High Street yesterday when she had thought he was away. His father had postponed their holiday for a few days to conduct the funeral of an old friend on Monday, and as soon as she heard this she had asked him to come to their barbecue tonight and promised to tell him about their adventure at Pollards and Conways. He was in a hurry on an errand for his mother, but he'd promised to come to the party if he could, and that he would look in at the *Blackbirds* in the morning to wish Mrs. Brown many happy returns. Lucy liked Mark very much. He had introduced her to country life and the wonders of nature, and never been impatient because everything was so strange to her. And what was more he had gone out of his way—as had his parents—to help her father and mother in their new life. So Mark was something special about this particular Saturday.

It had taken the combined efforts of her husband and two children to persuade Mrs. Brown to agree to the barbecue party. She finally gave way when Lucy had again told her how kind the Strangs and the Hogbens had been to them and how much she wanted her mother to meet Mrs. Strang. So both these families had been telephoned from Win Robson's greengrocer's shop a few steps further down Pottery Lane, and even Mr. Hogben had promised to come with the rest of his family, and this, Peggy had told Lucy, was the event of the year.

Later yesterday morning, when Humf had insisted on going shopping by himself, Lucy had remembered what P.C. Harris had hinted about Dandy and the Maycock family when he had brought them home in the panda car on Thursday evening. First she had gone to the police station to ask for the Maycocks' address. She had found Betsy and her mother at home, and although Dandy was out on duty with his handler she was introduced to the boisterous Nipper. She hadn't much time, but explained that she wanted a secret surprise for Humf and her mother and hoped that they would all come with Dandy to the barbecue. Betsy was thrilled, and before Mrs. Maycock could intervene, said that her father would be off duty on Saturday and she was sure he would like to bring Dandy. They had heard about Humf's adventures in the forest, but Mrs. Maycock asked whether Mrs. Brown would really like the idea and did she know that Lucy had asked them? Lucy was sure that her mother would be delighted, and eventually it was arranged that Betsy should come up to the *Blackbirds* after breakfast on Saturday to tell them if the sergeant would bring Dandy.

So this was something else which would be fun, and Lucy knew that she must choose the right moment to tell her mother before Betsy arrived and when Humf was out of the way.

The patch of sunlight had moved now across the ceiling, spot-lighting a tributary of the bigger river, and the sparrows were still scuffling in the gutter when the church clock announced the half hour. Lucy raised herself cautiously on one elbow and listened to muffled sounds on the landing below. Surely her mother could not be getting up so early on her birthday morning? She had promised faithfully to stay in bed until her presents had been opened, and as Lucy was sure that her brother wouldn't move until he was forcibly wakened, the mysterious sounds must mean that her father was already about. Lucy wondered why? It would be unlike him to be so excited about his wife's birthday that he couldn't sleep, and her parents always made their early morning tea with an electric kettle in their bedroom. What was he up to now at half past six? She decided to go and see, rolled carefully out of bed and without waiting to put on a dressing gown opened her bedroom door which squeaked. There was no sound from Humf so she trod carefully down the steep stairs which led from the top landing to what Mervyn Brown had once described as the "Juniors Private Suite." The door of her parents' bedroom was ajar, and Lucy pushed it back a few inches and peeped in. Only her mother was in the big bed and Lucy suddenly felt a lump in her throat as she looked at her peacefully asleep with one hand under her cheek and her hair tousled on the pillow. She looked so young and pretty that Lucy longed to run to her, put her arms round her and beg her to stay like this for always. She withstood the temptation, but as she quietly closed the door and went down the next flight of stairs to their living room and kitchen, she wondered what it was like to be as old as her parents and to share as many worries—and, as her mother had once gently reminded her—so many joys.

Surprisingly, her father was not on this floor either so he must have gone down to the café. When Lucy reached the café floor, she realised that the door leading into their small yard was wide open. She stood still in the passage for a moment and then heard her father whistling to himself. He had a nice whistle but a restricted repertoire of tunes. This morning Lucy recognised something from Gilbert and Sullivan which signified that he was in a good mood even though it was so early in the morning.

So she walked out into the yard where the cobbles, damp with dew, were refreshingly cool to her bare feet. She had forgotten the great golden rose which rioted up the flint walls at the back of their old house but her father had not. He was standing in his pyjamas rather precariously on one of the stools from the café kitchen and trying to cut roses with a pair of scissors.

She stood and watched him until he pricked his fingers, dropped the scissors and muttered a word which fortunately she didn't hear. Then he dropped the rose too and saw her.

"Careful, Dad!" she shouted as the stool wobbled. "Wait for me and I'll help you. Are these for Mum?"

"Good morning, Lucinda. We have not yet lived here six months and never before have I known you to get out of bed in the morning without being called. Have you dared to go in and wake your mother?"

"Only peeped from the door, Dad. She's still asleep. I heard somebody moving and thought it might be you. Humf is still asleep."

"Thank God," Mervyn said fervently. "Yes—these are for your mother and you may certainly help me. I'm pleased to see you and must now disclose my secret. My revised gift for your mother is a most artistic black vase—or container as the woman in the shop assured me they are now called—in which these golden roses will look most attractive . . . Remind me to tell you one day the story of King Midas who had the most beautiful rose garden in all the world. One day he pleased one of the ancient gods and asked, as a reward, that everything he touched might turn to gold. And so it did, poor fellow."

"You have told us, Dad. He touched his lovely roses and they turned to gold and he realised they could never be as beautiful as the real ones—like these."

The stool wobbled again and Mervyn stepped down and kissed her cheek.

"You are a good girl, Lucy. You even remember what I read to you. Fetch the kitchen scissors and another chair and then we'll arrange the roses in the container—and take it up to your mother with the other parcels."

Lucy ran upstairs to put on a jersey over her pyjamas, and when she came down again and reported that all was quiet her father was sitting on the stool instead of standing on it.

"I have an idea, Lucinda. No doubt both of you have some presents wrapped up and ready for presentation? Good. I suggest that as we are in good time, we not only have early morning tea with your mother, but breakfast together later. The post comes about eight, and the longer we are able to keep your mother in bed this morning the better—I am determined that this shall be a day of relaxation for her."

Lucy was reasonably sure that there would be no chance whatever for her mother to relax on this day more than any other. Apart from responsibility for the café, preparations for the barbecue were essential, and none of them could do what she did on every working day with the same quiet efficiency.

All the same it was not yet seven, and enough roses to fill several bowls could be cut in ten minutes. And although breakfast on four trays in one small bedroom would be chaotic when combined with parcel openings, it would be fun.

"All right, Dad," she agreed. "Boiled eggs, toast and honey and instant coffee. I'll do it if you don't fuss me and I'll start as soon as we've done the roses. All you need do is to carry up the trays when I'm ready and in the meantime you give Mum your presents and have your tea with her as usual."

"Just what I was going to suggest, my dear. An excellent idea. I will hold your chair firmly while you snip off the roses."

This was soon done and when Mervyn proudly produced a beautiful black oval vase which he had hidden in a cardboard box in the kitchen, Lucy agreed that it was a lovely present and helped him to arrange the blooms. As soon as he had gone upstairs, holding the vase in front of him as if it was a bomb likely to explode if roughly treated, Lucy laid four trays and then went up to dress and to wake her brother. Ten minutes later she was washed and dressed and having made sure that her present for her mother was still safe in the drawer of her dressing table, she went to wake Humf. To her surprise he was sitting up in bed with a small, square parcel wrapped in brown paper in his hands.

"Go away," he said in his surprisingly deep voice. "And please stay away. Can't I be privitt? Why can't you let me alone? And why are you dressed? Do you mean that the party has started in Mum's room and you didn't call me?"

Lucy closed the door and leaned against it.

"You're rude, Humf. Rude before you know what I've got to tell you. Hurry and get dressed and come and help me in the kitchen. We're all going to have a breakfast picnic in Mum's room and you can make the toast . . . Humf! What's in that parcel? It looks like a picture. Have you given Mum a picture because if you have so have I and that's awful . . ."

"What's your picture of?" Humf asked suspiciously.

"I'd better tell you now, I s'pose. It's an old picture, called a print, of Malling after a snowstorm. I found it in that old junk shop down by the station. What have you got?"

"I'm not going to show you yet but it's a sort of picture—more of a motto actually. Old-fashioned too but the man said it was very valuable and he let me have it very reasonable. So not to worry, Sis. Just go away and I'll come down and do the toast for you. Trouble about your idea is that you can't get much food at the same time on those trays and I tell you now I'm not going to keep running up and down those stairs. I'm not your slave, Sis, and I can't forget my wound in Deadman's Wood. I got to be careful of my foot. It would spoil Mum's birthday if I had to go to hospital again."

"Silly little boy, and don't call me Sis," Lucy laughed as she went out and closed the door. She was tempted to look in and greet her mother but realised that this wouldn't be fair to Humf, and there wasn't much time to waste if she insisted on being downstairs to open the café.

Lucy had long ago learned that even a simple breakfast will be a failure if the cook tries to do everything at once. She was still putting butter and marmalade in individual little saucers on each of the trays when the doorbell rang and she ran to take in a pile of letters and two parcels from the postman who said:

"Many happy returns to someone in this house. 'Morning, Lucy."

She took the mail back to the kitchen and a few minutes later her father, dressed and shaved, appeared.

"I'll take her letters up first, Lucy, and then help

with the trays. The container and the roses are a success. What are you and Humf giving her?"

"Antiques," Lucy laughed. "But not snuff-boxes! We haven't shown each other what we bought . . . Dad, I've got another surprise to tell you about though. You must promise not to tell Humf, although we may have to tell Mum before the party this evening . . . I've asked three other people and Dandy the police dog who rescued Humf. I want Dandy to be a surprise for him. I've invited Sergeant Maycock who is Dandy's handler, and Mrs. Maycock and Betsy who is our friend at school. Betsy is coming up after breakfast to tell us if her father will bring the dog. You don't mind, do you?"

Mervyn clapped his hands to his balding forehead. "*Must* we tell your mother, Lucy? She thinks we've got too many now. She's in a tizzy. Thinks we won't have enough food. How many now, Lucy? Four of us, four Hogbens, two Strangs. That's ten."

"And Mark, Dad. He's coming, I hope, but his parents can't. He said something about bringing them into the café this morning to see Mum."

"That's eleven, then. And now you want a policeman, a policeman's wife and child and a DOG!"

Lucy nodded. She didn't dare tell her father it might be two dogs because Betsy would certainly bring her disreputable puppy.

"Very well, my dear. I must face this crisis. We must all work together because I will not have your mother worried on this day of all days . . . Now for breakfast and the presentations . . . Good morning, Humphrey. Take up your own tray, if you please. Boiled eggs, toast and coffee to follow and you can leave that to me. I shall be interested to know what you have got for your mother."

Humf smirked and picked up a tray.

"Surprise for you too, Dad. And for Lucy. I've done a special card for Mum. A king-size card. Big as a poster. I want some of that sticky tape stuff please to fix it on Mum's wardrobe."

The birthday breakfast was a hilarious success. Mrs. Brown never for a moment showed any of them that she would have preferred to be up and organising and feeding her family. In a few moments, after Lucy and Humf had kissed her and sung "Happy Birthday" her bedroom was in chaos. The bed was covered with envelopes, birthday cards, letters and wrappings. Her roses were on the dressing table and the only place for the trays was under the bed until the rubbish had been cleared away. Humf's birthday card was a masterpiece —"Art" was his favourite subject at school. On a large sheet of white paper he had drawn a frieze of strutting blackbirds with yellow bills, both top and bottom of the paper, and in between he had sketched in different coloured inks this message:

BIRTHDAY GREETINGS
to OUR MUM
from the youngest
Blackbird
in the nest
signed: Humf Mervyn Brown

"I hope you won't mind, Mum," he said as he stepped back and bumped into the bed while surveying his handiwork. "I hope you'll like it, but my other present what I bought yesterday is another message but smaller to put on your mantelpiece. It's very old and very rare and valuable."

As her mother tore off the brown paper and looked

at what he had given her, Lucy saw tears in her eyes. His present was a small framed motto embellished with a rather crude coloured sketch of a sundial in a garden in which hollyhocks were growing in abundance. The greeting was headed "With love to Mother" and the first of three verses read:

Mother dear, whose life, to me
A constant joy has been,
I give you thanks for all the years
Of happiness I've seen.

"Oh, Humf darling," she said in a chokey voice as she hugged him. "Thank you so much. Put it on the mantelpiece now and it shall always stay there. Now, I want Lucy's present please before I open anything else."

Lucy had felt a little jealous of Humf's gifts—she had known nothing about the giant birthday card—but she needn't have worried. The engraving of Malling under snow was much admired and Mervyn, as well as her mother, congratulated her on her choice, and indeed some years later the picture proved to be valuable.

Then the other greetings were opened. A comic card from the Hogbens and something more artistic from the rector and Mrs. Simson. A card showing wild geese in flight from their son Mark, and other letters from relations and a few old friends in Midchester which pleased Mrs. Brown very much. After half an hour of excitement she sent them all out of the room while she tidied up and they cooked the breakfast. There wasn't really room for them to eat but Humf had his tray on the floor, Lucy on the end of her mother's bed, and

Mervyn standing up at the chest of drawers he used as a dressing-table. Nobody complained that the eggs he had boiled were as hard as bullets or that Humf's toast was slightly scorched, and they were still eating and chattering when the doorbell rang insistently.

"Elsie!" Mrs. Brown gasped. "It must be! Look at the time. Nine o'clock. I shouldn't have stayed here so long. It's not fair to Elsie. Please let her in, Lucy, and explain that I won't be long. Now all of you run away and let me dress."

That morning at the *Blackbirds* was the most exciting since the day on which the café was opened. Elsie was in a wonderful mood. She brought Mrs. Brown an enormous bunch of sweet peas with birthday greetings which included the name of her young man, Bill, who had known them all since the day the café had opened. A few minutes after Elsie, Win Robson from the greengrocer's shop arrived with a box of peaches and would not disclose who had told her that this particular Saturday was a birthday.

As soon as Mrs. Brown came down to the café she took control. First she warned Elsie that they might be extra busy today and then turned her husband and children out of the kitchen.

"I'm not doing anything about the barbecue, Mervyn. That is your affair. I'm going to sit back and be waited on. I've stopped worrying about it but I can still see that you haven't. Take the children away with you and leave Elsie and me in peace. Be off with you all."

Lucy soon realised that her father was in one of his states, so she took him up to their living room and helped him with his calculations for sausages, bags of crisps, rolls and cheese.

"And Dad, when you've got this grill for the

barbecue what are you going to do about a fire? How are you going to cook the bangers?"

"My dear child! Surely you know me well enough to realise that I have prepared for every eventuality! The fire will be of driftwood of course. Gathering it together will be part of the fun. You, Humphrey, can imagine yourself as a shipwrecked mariner cast up on a lonely beach."

Humf was unimpressed.

"How you going to light damp driftwood, Dad? We'll want a lot of matches."

"Obviously, Humphrey. I had this problem at the back of my mind. Add matches to the list, Lucy."

"And firelighters, Dad. We'd better have a packet of them and somebody told me that you must have charcoal on a barbecue . . . I'll put it down."

Then Elsie put her head round the door.

"Visitor for you, Lucy. You'd better come down."

Lucy hoped for Mark but was pleased to see Betsy and wondered whether she had introduced herself to her mother. She hadn't, as Mrs. Brown was busy in her kitchen.

Lucy sat her down at the table nearest the door.

"Is it O.K., Betsy? Can your father bring Dandy?"

"Yes—and Mum said to ask your mum if it's O.K. for so many——"

"Not so loud, Betsy! This is to be a surprise for Humf, but I've spoken to Dad who is organising the party and he said you're very, very welcome. My dad is keen on the police and we'd love to have you—'bout seven o'clock we'll be there."

"There's something else I forgot to tell you yesterday, Lucy. I've had a bit of an adventure too. Would you like to know? It's not like Humf's adventure, of course, but when I told Dad last night when I was asking him about tonight he was a bit cross I hadn't told him on Thursday, but I forgot."

"Tell me, Betsy. I'll walk down Pottery Lane with you."

Betsy's story didn't take long but it reminded Lucy of events she had been trying to forget.

"It all started with Nipper, Lucy. On Thursday afternoon Mum took me down to Greenhaven and we both had a swim. After, while she was sitting in the sun, I took Nipper for a walk up by that caravan camp and met a nice artist woman. She was painting pictures for postcards and was friendly with Nipper and talked to me about painting. I liked her. Very sort of artistic she was with black hair and big earrings. She said she was going on somewhere else in her caravan and I said she ought to come and paint here in Malling."

"What happened then? Where's the adventure?"

"That was all, really, except that I mentioned it to Dad last night and he suddenly got a bit excited and asked whether I'd seen a man with her like the man you saw in the forest. I said 'No' and he was cross again when I couldn't remember the number of her car, but of course I didn't see it 'cos it was parked with her caravan further up the hill. Then Dad said they were looking for a woman who had been going about asking to paint pictures of houses but I remembered this one's name. It was Elizabeth Sandford, so I told Dad that. So it was a small adventure, wasn't it?"

Lucy agreed, but she didn't say anything about the warning the police had given her mother and the farmers about a grey-haired woman hiker. They didn't sound like the same person but they might be. So she said "See you soon" to Betsy and ran up the hill again just in time to catch Mark on the doorstep of the *Blackbirds*.

He brought more flowers for Mrs. Brown and a message from his parents that they would like a table reserved for lunch and would wish her "Happy Birthday" then. They were sorry that they couldn't come to the party but offered to give the Browns a lift this evening in their old car with all the provisions. This was just the sort of thing that the vicar was always doing for people, and Mrs. Brown accepted gratefully. Mark then sat down in the café and invited Lucy to an ice and while they were enjoying these she told him about their adventure in the forest. She was still talking when some more people came in for coffee, so they went out into the castle grounds and she found herself telling him all about the snuff-box and Betsy's story about the woman artist.

As usual Mark was a good listener.

"Poor Lucy," he said when she had finished. "Bad luck for your father about the snuff-box and rotten for you to get mixed up in it like that. Wish I'd been with you at Pollards . . . Never mind. We'll see John and Peggy tonight at your party and try to fix another camp when I come back . . . You're still worried about that man on the run, aren't you?"

"I can't forget him, Mark. I don't like anybody or anything being hunted. And now there's this business of Betsy's woman artist."

"You mean she may be the same woman as the grey-haired one the police were looking for? So she might, Lucy. Any woman can wear a wig in these days. My father says he can't keep up with all these changes. Sometimes he thinks he's got somebody new in the congregation and when he tries to welcome a stranger at the door after service, he realises it's Mrs. Snooks or somebody who's been coming to church for years . . . I must go now. I'll be in the café to lunch with the parents and we'll see you tonight soon after six. I wonder what sort of a time Humf is having out shopping with your father? Cheerio!"

The next excitement was the return of the two Brown males. From somewhere Mr. Brown had borrowed a shopping trolley while Humf was laden with the portable barbecue which consisted of an iron tray on folding metal legs and a grill which fitted into it and on which the meat would rest.

"Nothing now for you to worry about, my dear," Mervyn explained to his wife. "I shall have a further check this afternoon but all purchases have been made successfully. Is all going well here? I'm sorry I can't be in two places at once but I shall be at your service in a few minutes. I do hope you are having a happy birthday my dear?"

They told him of the vicar's promise of transport this evening, and then Mrs. Brown gently pointed out that the borrowed grill was only large enough to cook sausages for about six people at a time, and that they were not likely to find any driftwood small enough to go into the metal tray.

"Quite so, my dear. Please don't concern yourself about these trifles. Humphrey and I have a supply of firelighters and charcoal and shall be prepared for every eventuality."

"I'm sure you will, Mervyn. You may take a roll of my oven foil and there is some fine mesh chicken wire in the yard which I'm sure you'll be able to fix above a much bigger driftwood fire . . . Elsie and I are managing very well and I'd be glad if you'd leave us alone in the kitchen. We'll call you if we want help."

The café was full for two hours at lunch time. The Simsons came as promised and everything went well. Elsie took the orders and waited, Mrs. Brown cooked and Mervyn washed up without breaking anything. Soon after two o'clock, when the last customer had gone, Mrs. Brown insisted that Elsie should go home for a rest and then sat down with her family in the café to have their own meal when a panda car drew up outside. Humf left his favourite meal of fried eggs and baked beans and ran out to meet his colleagues.

"Your mother and father in, Humf?" P.C. Harris asked as he got out. "Shan't keep them long but I've news for them—and for you and Lucy."

"You come in right now. And Robert too if he can. Come and have some baked beans. They're super here . . . Have you got that man? Has Dandy found him?"

The constable put his hand on the boy's shoulder and followed him into the café.

"Sergeant asked me to tell you that the woman we want has been found in a caravan camp near Chichester," he explained after greeting the others. "Calls herself Elizabeth Sandford and she's now helping us with our enquiries. We've heard that under the wig she was wearing, her grey hair is cropped short."

"But the man? The frightened man? Have you found him yet?"

"No, Lucy. Not yet. Miss Sandford may help us to find him . . . No, thank you, Mrs. Brown. I can't stay now but we wanted you all to know as you've been so helpful. We did hear down at the station that there's an important birthday in this house today and Humf's friends wish you many happy returns, Mrs. Brown. And so no more worries about women artists and hikers . . . Sorry, Humf. I haven't seen Dandy today. Maybe it's his day off."

Humf went out to see the panda off and when he came back none of the others had much to say. Truth was of course that they had all forgotten about crime and criminals and didn't like to be reminded of it today. So Humf had the sense to keep quiet too, and they were all surprised when Mrs. Brown agreed to her husband's suggestion that she should go upstairs and rest while they looked after the café until Elsie returned.

At half-past six Mr. Simson and Mark arrived in their car. The boot was crammed with food, the small grill, the chicken wire and oven foil, cutlery from the café, cardboard plates and plastic mugs, thermos flasks of coffee and, following a later appeal from Humf, a case of cans of soft drinks.

Lucy was pale with excitement and her father nervously talkative. The calmest of them all was the chief guest who settled herself in the front seat next to the vicar while the others fussed about behind them.

The journey to the end of the track which led down between the cliffs to Smugglers Cove took only half an hour. When they drove into the rough car park, Lucy recognised the Strangs' car and by the time they had unpacked, the Hogbens arrived in their Land Rover. They had also been told about Miss Sandford.

"We'll waste no time talking about that woman." Mrs. Hogben said after she had warmly embraced Mrs. Brown and wished her many happy returns. "I've always enjoyed a good party and I'm going to make the best of this one. And so is my husband, although he always pretends he hasn't got time for anything except work. Now, my dear, I hope you won't mind but I happened to be using the oven this morning and I thought maybe that nice cold steak and kidney pie might make a change at a picnic. I wasn't sure how many you were having—I rang up Mrs. Strang and she didn't know either but she's brought some of their own tomatoes—so while I was about it I made a medium-sized one. John will carry it down for us."

Humf's eyes widened expectantly as he saw what the Hogbens meant by medium-sized. Although John played the fool by pretending that he couldn't lift the enormous pie dish, everybody else made appreciative noises of thanks. As the Strangs were already on the beach, Lucy suggested that she go ahead with her mother to welcome them.

"And it's no good looking at me like that, John and Peggy. I'm not trying to get out of carrying my share. It's our party so we shouldn't keep them waiting. You others come as quickly as you can."

Ever since Lucy had thought of asking the Maycocks and Dandy, she wanted their appearance to be a complete surprise. Although she was tempted now to warn her mother that something exciting was still to happen, she decided to hurry ahead with her heavy basket and hope that she would be as pleased as Humf when they did come.

"You'll like Mr. and Mrs. Strang, Mum. I know you will. Humf will tell you again how kind they were to us and I'll tell them now that we're all on our way."

Lucy had only been once before to Smugglers Cove. Mark had taken her one winter's day when great waves were pounding up the rocky beach in a flurry of spray which tasted salt on her lips. She remembered how they had to shout to each other to be heard above the noise of the wind and the sea. He had told her that seals had been seen here sometimes and that it was dangerous to picnic right under the cliffs as lumps of chalk often tumbled to the beach in winter. He had promised to take her shrimping here when the tide was low one day in the summer, and now half the summer had flown already, and shrimping was something else to look forward to when Mark came back from his holiday.

She remembered that the only way down to the

beach between the cliffs was by a flight of narrow concrete steps, and when she reached them tonight she put her basket down, stood for a moment at the top and saw that the tide was out and the sea calm in the evening light. Two couples were shrimping in the rock pools and away on the horizon were some fishing boats.

She glanced back and waved to her mother and Humf who were just in sight and then scrambled down the steps. Half way down she saw, about fifty yards on her left, a huge, smooth lump of rock on the top of which a woman was sitting as she looked out to sea. Above her the gulls swooped and hovered and below her, on the cliff side of the beach a man was unpacking a haversack. How like Mrs. Strang to sit quietly while her husband did something practical!

Lucy shouted and waved and some gulls at the edge of a pool took flight. Mrs. Strang heard her first and raised her hand.

Mr. Strang greeted her affectionately and when Lucy explained that the others would soon be here, she told them about the Maycocks and Dandy and then about Miss Sandford.

"The police telephoned us about her, Lucinda, and now we must forget her. No news of the unfortunate young man so we can forget about him too and enjoy ourselves. I hope your father won't mind but I have had some experience of camp fires and I was planning to start one here between these rocks. The wind is blowing from the west, so we shall sit this side where there is a patch of smooth sand. We are looking forward to meeting your parents, Lucinda, and here if I am not mistaken is Humphrey and your mother. Don't worry, we shall not mention the Maycocks."

From that moment the party was a success. Mrs. Strang made a graceful descent from her rock and within a few minutes was talking to Mrs. Brown as if she had known her for months. Mervyn was in fine form and had no objection to following Mr. Strang's advice about the fire and proudly produced his chicken wire and foil. The children were sent to hunt for driftwood and came back laden, and Humf was allowed to have his own barbecue on the small grill. He was just blowing the flames from the firelighter on to the lumps of charcoal in the metal tray when Lucy ran down to him.

"Look, Humf! That's Betsy Maycock coming down the steps with her puppy . . . And Humf—look who's behind her. Surely that's Dandy and the Sergeant and Mrs. Maycock? I asked them to the party Humf and had to keep it a secret from you and Mum until they came. Run and meet them."

The smile he gave her was sufficient reward, and as he raced across the beach Lucy turned to her mother and explained what she had done and why.

"That was a lovely idea, Lucy. I'm having such a happy day and I shall be so pleased to know the Maycocks. I'll come with you now to meet them . . . What a beautiful dog . . ."

Humf was now on his knees with his arms round Dandy's neck. The dog's tail was waving gently and as Lucy and her mother came up he turned to look at his master as if asking permission to be a domestic dog for a few hours.

Lucy and Humf hardly recognised the sergeant out of uniform but it was soon obvious the Maycocks would fit in with the others.

The men got two fires going and as soon as the flames—coloured strangely blue and green from the salt in the driftwood—died down, sausages were frizzling on the foil above the glowing embers. The three wives cut and buttered rolls and set out mugs and plates on a big plastic sheet brought by Mrs. Hogben.

Mrs. Strang's tomatoes were very welcome and Mrs. Maycock had brought big potatoes to roast in the ashes. Mervyn, to everyone's delight put on a chef's white hat and a striped apron but in spite of the uniform he upset a pan of potato crisps and almost stepped back on to the barbecue where Humf and Betsy were working amicably together with their own sausages.

While the preparations were going on, Nipper, Betsy's puppy was rather a nuisance, but sat close to Humf with his nose twitching at the smell of cooking.

Slowly the sun went down and the first stars twinkled in the east. John, Peggy and Mark wandered off to see how the shrimpers were getting on. Mr. Hogben lay back on the sand, smoked his pipe and thought of his harvest ripening in his fields a few miles away. Lucy sat down next to Mrs. Strang not only because she had not as much to say as the others, but because she liked her so much. And then her mother came over to join them and asked about Pollards and told her how grateful she and Mervyn were over their care of the children. Mr. Strang was quietly efficient and talked to the sergeant about the smugglers who once used this beach for landing brandy and lace from France.

And then they started what Humf called the banquet. They sang 'Happy Birthday' again and drank Mrs. Brown's health. They burned their fingers and sucked off the grease. Nobody, not even Mervyn, mentioned the snuff-box because it was still with the police, and as the twilight deepened they saw one of the big French Car Ferries out from Newhaven on its way to Dieppe with all lights blazing. And then the moon came up—a great fat, golden, harvest moon which made a glittering path across the darkening water.

Once, a silence was broken by Mervyn who asked Sergeant Maycock what he thought had happened to the unfortunate young man who had started all the trouble when he walked into the *Blackbirds* only a few days ago.

"We shall find him eventually. He's probably been stealing small things on the quiet since we missed him in the forest on Thursday. Although he knows we're looking for him he might not be far away and we may search the forest again tomorrow. He may believe that we won't look round here because we think he would be sure to try and get further away. We can't be sure but I don't reckon he's very bright. Poor type really and no match for our Miss Sandford."

"I expect he's hungry by now," Lucy said quietly. "Let's not talk about him."

The sergeant gave her a sympathetic smile and then suddenly turned to Humf.

"Hi there, young man. Don't let me ever catch you offering any sort of food to Dandy. He's been trained only to take food from me or the family. Nobody else ever. Not even you. If he takes food from anybody else he might take poison one day like the dogs at Pollards and Conways. See what I mean? Make a fuss of him whenever you meet if you like, but never feed him."

Humf looked abashed and stood up.

"I'll remember, sir. Sorry. May I take him for a walk now with Betsy. I want to explore round the cliff there. Where we can't see. I bet there are all sorts of smugglers' haunts round there . . . And please don't tell us to be careful, Mum. Dandy will look after us."

The sergeant looked at Mervyn and then nodded.

"O.K. then. Don't go too far and don't walk right under the cliffs. Leave the pup with your mother, Betsy."

He clicked his tongue at Dandy who came to him

obediently. None of them heard what he said to the dog who turned at once and stood between the two children.

"Cheerio all, then," Humf said as he put his hand on Dandy's head. "We just want to see where those old smugglers hid their stuff. Shan't be long."

"Keep out of the caves. They're not safe," Mr. Strang warned them, and when they were out of ear-shot he turned to Mark and Lucy.

"Keep an eye on them," he suggested. "Tide won't be up for two hours but they might get into trouble. And but for the moon it will be dark soon."

John who was helping his sister to pack up called after them, "We'll be along in a sec. I suppose if you gave that dog a net he'd soon find us a bucketful of shrimps!"

"Had a good day, Lucy? I'm sure your mother has," Mark said as they climbed over the rocks and shingle towards the great chalk cliff round which Humf, Betsy and Dandy had just disappeared. "I wish my parents could have come. They like yours, you know. So do I. Your father makes me laugh. Tell me again about this incredible dog and how he found Humf in the forest. Wish I'd been with you."

Lucy said that she wished he had too and then, as they found themselves in the next cove, they saw Humf and Betsy only about twenty yards away. Mark called, "Wait for us," and when they joined them and had patted Dandy who obviously didn't think much of stony beaches and the smell of seaweed, Humf made his protest.

"Trouble with you lot is that you can't let me have any private life. Why must you follow me round?"

They looked at him in astonishment and at that moment Dandy cocked his ears and growled a warning.

"Be quiet," Betsy whispered as the dog looked towards a big rock on the other side of the pool by which they were standing. For several long, long moments there was no sound but the murmur of the sea and their own breathing. The light was fading fast as from behind the rock only about ten yards away there stepped a thin, bedraggled young man. It was too dark to see his features but Lucy knew him at once.

With one hand on the rock he stared at them, muttering words they could not understand. Then he stooped and picked up a big stone in his right hand.

"You're the dog poisoner! You're the man the police want," Humf shouted hysterically.

The man stepped forward. "Get out all of you," he yelled. "Take that dog away. This is my private beach." Then, more quietly, almost wheedling, in a voice which made Lucy feel sick, "Listen. I'm hungry and thirsty. I must have food. Go and fetch me something to eat. Meat I want. Not raw fish. I'll pay you for it . . . *But take that dog away*."

None of them moved nor answered, but as Dandy's growl turned to a snarl the man made his terrible mistake. He swung his arm back to hurl the stone, but before it could leave his hand Dandy had leapt the pool and was at him. As he had been trained to do, the dog seized his right forearm. Jasper dropped the stone with a scream of terror and as he stumbled to the ground Betsy flung her arms round Dandy and shouted:

"Keep still and he won't hurt you. Don't move." She knew what would happen if he struggled and that she could not prevent Dandy from mauling him if he tried to attack any of them.

Then the dog, obedient to his training, lifted his head and barked again and again so that the sound of his triumph echoed back from the cliffs and some startled gulls rose into the dusk squawking in protest.

"Run for Sergeant Maycock, Mark," Lucy begged. Quickly the boy obeyed and the man on the ground whimpered with terror while the great dog stood guard over him. Humf turned for comfort to his sister who was looking disgusted. He no longer felt like a great detective or even a dog handler, but only like a small boy who, never before, had seen a man frightened for his life.

Then Betsy stood up and whispered, "Dad will come. He can hear Dandy. We must stay until he arrives."

So they stood in silence until the sergeant came running to them across the rough beach with John and Peggy not far behind him. He nodded to the children, praised the dog and patted him and then hauled the frightened man to his feet.

"Come along, matey. We've been looking for you. Been hiding in the caves I shouldn't be surprised, but now you're hungry . . . We'll soon see about that . . . You kids run back now and see if there's any food left. Hot coffee would be useful and tell the ladies what's to do . . . Off you go . . . You're safe enough now, matey. The dog won't touch you, unless you get ideas about running off . . ."

Then the other three men, who had met the children running back, arrived but the only one to speak was Mervyn.

"Yes, Sergeant," he said quietly. "That's the chap who sold me the snuff-box. What a fool I was . . . and so was he."

And that is almost the end of Mrs. Brown's birthday party and of this story. By the time the sergeant, Jasper and the others reached the camp the boys had flung more wood on the glowing embers of the fire and the flames leapt high. Mrs. Hogben looked at the miserable Jasper and then at her husband.

"Poor fellow. He's starving. That's the chap who came asking for a job and stole my snuff-box. Give him what's left of my steak pie, Sergeant, and there's some coffee in that flask . . . We'll get moving now and arrange some transport. Hogbens first as we're nearest home."

The children turned away when they saw how Jasper attacked the food. Nobody had much to say but they heard Mr. Hogben promise the sergeant to telephone the police with the news that Jasper had been found and ask for a patrol car, and then to come back for the Browns and Mark and take them home. The Strangs then suggested that Mrs. Maycock and Betsy should come with them and be dropped in Malling on the way.

And so the party broke up, while the sergeant with Dandy at his side sat with Jasper by the camp fire.

"Come down to the sea with me," Mrs. Brown said suddenly. "Mark as well. We'll wait there in the moonlight until the Hogbens come back for us. Say good night to Dandy, Humf. You'll see him again . . . Good night, Sergeant, and thank you for coming to my party and for all your help."

She took Lucy's hand and as they turned away Humf went up to the dog. For once he could find no words as he stroked Dandy's head and felt it suddenly pressed against his thigh. With shame he felt tears in his eyes and the sergeant's voice sounded a little husky as he said:

"He won't forget you, son. Come home and see him whenever you like. You and your sister will always be welcome . . . Good night and thanks for your help."

The dog moved so that he could lick the boy's hand, and as Humf stooped so that his cheek was against his head he knew that there was only one thing to say:

"Good dog," he whispered. "Good dog, Dandy!"

GOOD DOG DANDY is the second book in the Brown Family series, and was written especially for Armada. It follows THE SECRET OF GALLEYBIRD PIT.

The author hopes that you have enjoyed this story and would like to know what you think of it. You can write to him, and, if you live in the United Kingdom or Eire, he will answer your letter, which should be addressed to:

Malcolm Saville,
c/o Armada Books,
14 St. James's Place,
London, SW1A 1PF.

Have you read Malcolm Saville's Lone Pine Adventure stories?

Each adventure is complete in itself and there are now nineteen of them. The complete list is as follows:

1. MYSTERY AT WITCHEND
2. SEVEN WHITE GATES
3. THE GAY DOLPHIN ADVENTURE
4. THE SECRET OF GREY WALLS
5. LONE PINE FIVE
6. THE ELUSIVE GRASSHOPPER
7. THE NEGLECTED MOUNTAIN
8. SAUCERS OVER THE MOOR
9. WINGS OVER WITCHEND
10. LONE PINE LONDON
11. THE SECRET OF THE GORGE
12. MYSTERY MINE
13. SEA WITCH COMES HOME
14. NOT SCARLET BUT GOLD
15. TREASURE AT AMORYS
16. MAN WITH THREE FINGERS
17. RYE ROYAL
18. STRANGERS AT WITCHEND
19. WHERE'S MY GIRL?